The Collector's Catalogue

of

BRUSH - McCOY POTTERY

An identification Guide for over
1,100 pieces of J. W. McCoy
and
Brush - McCoy Pottery

by

Sharon and Bob Huxford

COLLECTOR BOOKS

Additional copies of this book may be ordered from:

COLLECTOR BOOKS
P.O. Box 3009
Paducah, Kentucky 42001

or

Mr. and Mrs. Bob Huxford
1202 Seventh Street
Covington, Indiana 47932
@ $7.95 Postpaid

ACKNOWLEDGEMENTS

We wish to express our most sincere gratitude to

Lucile (Brush) and Clare Barnett

and

Billie and Nelson McCoy, Jr.

The combined interests and energies implied by the old company name "The Brush-McCoy Pottery" have been retained in some aspects to the present by the descendants of these two great leaders of the industry who are rightly proud of their inheritance - they share a common goal, that of preserving as much of the history of that giant pottery as they are able to collect. Through their kind generosity we were permitted to reproduce these old company catalogues, without which it would have been an impossible task to properly present to collectors an accurate listing of the lines of manufacture.

We know you will find each turn of these pages tremendously exciting and informative, and will, we are sure, want to join with us in thanking them for revealing to us all this delightful new field of art pottery.

ABOUT THE HUXFORDS

As a result of their shared enthusiasm for collecting a wide variety of both glass and pottery for nearly ten years, Sharon and Bob have become not only collectors, but researchers as well--a field they both agree is most exciting for them. After their first two books were published (*The Story of Fiesta, The Collectors Encyclopedia of Fiesta*) they began to concentrate their interests on the Ohio art potteries. In 1976 their book *"The Collectors Encyclopedia of Roseville Pottery"* was published, and was followed shortly afterward with *"The Collectors Catalogue of Early Roseville"*. Most recently completed, *"The Collectors Encyclopedia of McCoy Pottery"* is a companion to this book. They are presently involved in reconstructing the history of the Brush Pottery Company which they feel will complete this study.

They have written articles for both *"The Depression Glass Daze"* and *"The Glaze"*, and have been named pottery editors for Collector Books.

3

INTRODUCTION

The pottery from whose catalogues the following pages have been reproduced was incorporated on September 5, 1899, under the name of the J. W. McCoy Pottery Company, after the founder and first president. The original papers of incorporation were issued by the state of West Virginia who claimed to be the "most liberal state in the union", and whose fee for out of state applicants was a mere $62.00, attorney's fee included---no personal checks accepted!

It was an era when men saw in the abundant clay fields and easily accessible coal deposits a golden opportunity to turn their investments into wealth. Those with the means to establish even a small business were welcomed into the area and encouraged to take part in its development. The opening of a new pottery was a social event frequently celebrated with parties and dances attended by prominent members of the community.

Although there were scores upon scores of potteries which operated briefly, there were many that developed into giant industries, prospered and continued for many years to produce various types of wares from the high quality Ohio clays. For the most part, these giants have been extensively studied and collectors of art pottery intensively absorbed in searching for examples of their work; yet very little is known about the J. W. McCoy Pottery, even though its success is evidenced by the fact that the pottery that traces its genesis to this original organization still operates in the Roseville-Zanesville area of Ohio under the title "The Brush Pottery Company".

These catalogue pages unveil another art pottery field, of as yet uncertain scope, full of treasures yet to be discovered.

AN ABBREVIATED HISTORY OF THE POTTERY

History recalls only sketchy information about the early years of the pottery. No doubt their primary production concentrated heavily on domestic wares . . . bowls, pitchers, crocks and chambers; but soon they were producing more decorative pottery as well--majolica-type cuspidors, jardinieres and pedestals, and umbrella stands in a glaze they preferred to call "blended".

Although these lines were the "bread and butter" income of the many rival potteries in the Roseville-Zanesville area, many companies were attempting to capture the eyes of the public with their experiments in the art pottery field. Weller, then J.B. Owens and the Roseville Pottery were only a few vying for prominence in a market saturated with competition.

Perhaps the first art line to be conceived by the J.W. McCoy Pottery was Mt. Pelee. Introduced around 1902, much of it was lost in the fire that destroyed the Roseville plant in 1903. Examples of this unusual ware are very rarely found today. Marked Mt. Pelee in incised letters, moulded shapes were altered by hand, the wet clay pinched and pulled to form sharp crests. Further decoration was sometimes applied in an inventive, if not eccentric style. Some feel the line was inspired by ancient pottery discovered about that time in the ruins of St. Pierre, Isle of Martinique. Although the glaze most often reported is an iridescent charcoal grey, one marked piece is known to exist in green--and other colors may yet be discovered.

The company's 1904 catalogue had already gone to the printers, and so survived the 1903 fire. More than likely it was never used. It lists a line called Rosewood, and since a few pieces of this ware have been found, we assume it was being made prior to the fire. (Since the name Rosewood was used for a brown glazed line produced after the fire, more than likely the earlier Rosewood line had already been discontinued.) The early Rosewood was a standard brown glazed ware, offered in twelve vase shapes and decorated simply with diagonal orange brush strokes. Two large jardinieres were also shown in this line and prices were about double those of the blended lines.

In addition to Rosewood, the 1904 catalogue, a 4" x 9" black and white phamplet, depicts 38 pages of "Art and Glazed Ware, Jardinieres, Pedestals and Cuspidors". Their New York office address is listed as No. 42, West Broadway.

Their line was offered in some of the following blends and colors:

Light Blends: Blue, green, red and brown.
Carnelian: Brown, olive, blue and red.
Rainbow: Pink, brown, green and blue.

Prices ranged from $4.50 per dozen on small jardinieres to as much as $20.00 each for a jardiniere and pedestal with an overall height of 33".

The remaining pages show utility wares such as jugs, nested nappies in both a blue and gold finish and the green on ivory mottled glaze that remained a popular product with the company for years. Bake pans, stew kettles and a small 4" "Gem pan" with a wire handle were offered in "black lined or blue all over". The concluding pages show Bristol Toilet Sets, cuspidors and chambers; and a line of red burned flower pots and saucers.

By February 1, 1905, their new facilities were finished on Perry Street in Roseville; and with a substantially increased capitol, the company voted to become an Ohio Corporation. In July, the original West Virginia corporation was dissolved. Once again ready to venture into the realm of art pottery, the McCoy Company introduced a line of standard brown ware, with slip underglaze painting called Loy-Nel-Art, after J.W.'s three sons, Lloyd, Nelson, and Arthur. This line, although not always marked, carried in die-impressed letters the mark "Loy-Nel-Art, McCoy". These pieces are very rarely found artist signed, but two have been located, one signed "Chilcote" and the other T.S. (Tot Steel, who worked for Weller and Owens?) You will note on the catalogue pages that the price for Loy-Nel-Art was often the same as the price for a similar piece of matt green finished ware. One might assume, then, that McCoy artists were not over-paid for their talent, and that perhaps artists of a high caliber were not encouraged to work there. During this period, two other artistic lines of excellent quality were produced, decorated with garlands or wreaths of leaves and berries, or with floral applique in natural colors on a beautifully enduring high gloss brown glaze. The "cameo type" decorations are molded into the ware, and both share a common characteristic . . . some pieces will be found in each line with the diagonal orange streaks reminiscent of the very early Rosewood. Although no obvious differences can be cited between these lines, both carry their line name in incised lettering . . . Olympia, and Rosewood (to which we might add: second line).

In 1909 George S. Brush became General Manager of the pottery. His interest in the ceramic industry began in 1901 when he accepted a position with the J. B. Owens Pottery Company in Zanesville, Ohio as head of their printing department. Until 1905 he was reporter, printer, editor and publisher of *"The Owens Monthly"*. At that time, he became their sales manager, continuing with the Owens company until 1907, when he left to organize his own pottery. The Brush Pottery was a one-kiln operation in the Putnam section of Zanesville . . . one year later it was destroyed by fire.

In 1908, he became the manager of the Globe Stoneware Company and the Crooksville Clay Products Company; the next year began his association with the J. W. McCoy Pottery Company. On October 23, 1911 all three companies merged and became known as the Brush-McCoy Pottery Company. The President was W. R. Baker, and George S. Brush was General Manager. J. W. McCoy continued with the company as a principal stockholder. A second plant was acquired, that of the J. B. Owens Pottery Company, Plant No. 1, on Dearborn Street in Zanesville, where they made various lines of fine art pottery. They utilized the Owens Henri Deux molds and created the line they called Navarre. Their Oakwood line was developed from the style of some pottery left at the plant by Owens . . . their Mission line. During the next few years, art pottery was produced only in Zanesville, and the production of stoneware and cooking ware was confined to the Roseville plant.

On April 11, 1912, the company purchased "molds, saggers, established business and other items" from the A. Radford Pottery of Clarksburg, West Virginia, upon that firm's retirement. No doubt some of these molds were used by Brush-McCoy to produce their own lines--vases, for instance, presently in the storeroom of the Brush Pottery Company are molded along similar if not identical lines to some from the Radford Ruko and Thera lines--however, these lines were not reproduced by Brush-McCoy, these shapes were simply utilized and their own glazes and decorative methods applied.

During the next few years the pottery continued to prosper, and their ever-increasing capitol reflected a parallel climb in sales. Some of the J. W. McCoy lines continued to be produced, and new ones were offered continually, many of which were designed by A. L. Cusick, principal modeler with the pottery from 1908 until his death in January, 1946.

Three years before his association with J. W. McCoy, he and his partner, W. P. Jervis, had organized the Craven Art Pottery Company of East Liverpool, Ohio. Many of his designs show great attention to detail. His incised signature can be found on a few of these early pieces.

J. W. McCoy died in December, 1914, after an illness of three weeks. Cause of death was listed as Anemia. He was a highly respected leader of the community, and had contributed to its expansion in many ways. Aside from his work in the pottery industry, he was also a prominent merchant, having owned and operated a general store for several years in Roseville, Ohio. He was given much credit for promoting the educational program of the community. After his death, his interests in the pottery were carried out by his heirs.

In 1915, The Brush-McCoy Pottery adopted this identifying trademark: M-I-T-U-S-A. This was a composite of the first letter of each word in the phrase "Made in the United States (of) America. They continued to use this trademark until 1925.

After fire destroyed the manufacturing part of the Zanesville building in 1918, their Roseville plant was enlarged, several new gas kilns were added, and thereafter all production was contained at that location. However the offices and warehouse buildings in Zanesville continue in use to the present time. Still clearly visible on the old brick facade, white block letters announce "J. B. Owens, Plant No. 1", and for one split second transport the visitor backwards in time.

In 1925, the McCoy family withdrew their interests in the pottery.

George Brush served as President and General Manager until his death in 1934. He had played an important role in the progress of the pottery industry and had contributed much to the general development of the community as well.

By the late 1930's the market for the large vases and jardinieres had diminished, and the company turned to the production of novelties, planters, ash trays, etc. They also made a line of cookie jars which are attracting collectors today.

Descendants of both families still remain active in the production of pottery. Mr. W. Clare Barnett has been associated with the Brush Pottery since 1928, and has served as President and General Manager since 1955. His wife, Lucile, is the daughter of George Brush, and she presently holds the office of Secretary of the Company. J. W. McCoy's son, Nelson, founded the Nelson McCoy Sanitary Stoneware Company in Roseville, Ohio, in 1910, and his son, Nelson, is now President of that pottery, today operating under the title "The Nelson McCoy Pottery Company".

The first series of pictures, pages 9 through 32, are from the J. W. McCoy Pottery Company catalogue of 1910, which we have reproduced in its entirety. This was not necessarily the first year for some of these lines to be sold--for instance, on sheet P (page 18) the second umbrella stand, and the jardiniere and pedestal with the lion's head design (#2881) were shown in the 1904 catalogue. The Loy-Nel-Art line dates back four to five years previous, and so without doubt do others.

Pages 33 through 40 are from the Brush-McCoy catalogue of 1912-14. The cover shows the factories at both locations as they appeared at the peak of their productivity. Again, some of these lines were probably introduced sometime prior to 1912.

The three reprints on pages 41, 42, and 43 are from the 1915 catalogue; notice that some of the lines are repeated from earlier years. In the years that followed, the company began the practice of code-dating their catalogue pages -- for instance, Sheet 16-F is from 1916, Sheet 18-D from 1918, etc.

We guarantee there are surprises in store for you -- hold on to your seat!!!!

LOY-NEL HAND DECORATED UNDERGLAZE ART WARE.

No. 203 Jardiniere
7½ in. Loy-Nel Art. Dec. $11 25

No. 200 Jardiniere
8¼ in. Loy-Nel Art. Dec. $15 00

No. 201 Jardiniere
9¼ in. Loy-Nel Art. Dec. $19 25

No. 200 Jardiniere
10½ in. Loy-Nel Art. Dec. $21 50

No. 202 Jardiniere
12 in. Special Loy-Nel Art. Dec. $67 50

No. 1191 Jardiniere and Pedestal
12 in Jar 15 in. Pedestal. Loy-Nel Art.
Each. $5 95

No. 62 Umbrella Stand
22 in. Loy-Nel Art. 21 in. high, 9 in. opening. Each. $4 00

No. 112 Jardiniere
7½ in. Loy-Nel Art. Dec. $6 00

No. 96 Cut Flower Vase
Loy-Nel Art. Dec.

No. 96 Fern Dish
1 in. with liner, Dec. $5 00

No. 1 Cuspidor
7 in. Loy-Nel Art. Dec. $6 00

No. 60 Umbrella Stand
Loy-Nel Art. 17 in. high, 8 in. opening.
Each. $9 00

No. 2059 Jardiniere and Pedestal
Loy-Nel Art. 21 in. high, 12 in. Pedestal. Each. $6 00

SHEET G.

9

LOY-NEL ART WARE - HIGHEST GRADE

No. 70—Jardiniere
4 in. Jard. Loy-Nel Art. Doz.	$3.33
5 " " " "	5.00
6 " " " "	6.66
7 " " " "	10.00
8 " " " "	13.33
9 " " " "	16.66
10 " " " "	20.00

No. 70—Special
12 in. Wide at Top
16 in. Wide at Bulge
11½ in. High
Price $5.00 Each

No. 70—Mat Green Jardiniere
Same Price as Loy-Nel
Made in all sizes
including No. 70 Special

No. 2120 Jard. and Pedestal
Loy-Nel Art
7½ in. Jard. 8 in. Pedestal
Price $24.00 per Doz.

No. 212—Jardiniere only
7½ in. Loy-Nel Art. Doz. $9.00

No. 102—Cuspidor
Loy-Nel Art
8 in. Diameter
7 in. High
Price $10.00 Doz.

No. 102—Cuspidor
Mat Green
Price $10.00 Doz.

No. 114—Umbrella Stand
Loy-Nel Art
10 in. Opening
21 in. High
Price $5.00 Each

No. 114—Umbrella Stand
Mat Green
10 in. Opening
21 in. High
Price $5.00 Each

No.1190—Jard. and Pedestal
Loy-Nel Art
12 in. Jard. 18 in. Pedestal
$5.85 Each

No. 119—Jardiniere
10 in. Loy-Nel Doz. $20.00
12 " " " $30.00

No. 9—Vase
Loy-Nel Art
15½ in. High
8 in. Diameter
Price $3.50 Each

No. 7—Vase
Loy-Nel Art
10 in. High
11½ in. Diameter
Price $2.50 Each

No. 5—Vase
Loy-Nel Art
7½ in. High
7½ in. Diameter
Price $1.50 Each

No. 2—Vase
Loy-Nel Art
12 in. High
9 in. Diameter
Price $3.00 Each

No. 6—Vase
Loy-Nel Art
16 in. High
5½ in. Diameter
Price $3.00 Each

OUR SPECIAL---HIGH GRADE---FANCY VASES
NOTE PRICES

No. 66—Vase
Loy-Nel Art
6 in. High
Doz. $6.00

No. 64—Vase
Loy-Nel Art
8 in. High
Doz. $10.00

No. 63—Vase
Loy-Nel Art
10 in. High
Doz. $15.00

No. 62—Vase
Loy-Nel Art
12 in. High
Doz. $24.00

10

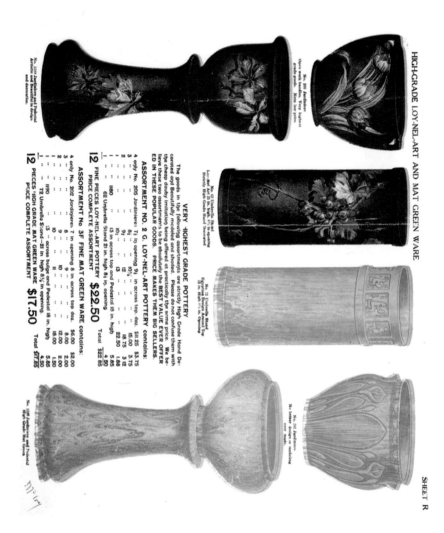

HIGH-GRADE LOY-NEL-ART AND MAT GREEN WARE

SHEET R

No. 1109 Jardiniere and Pedestal. Artistic and Beautiful design and decoration.

No. 205 Jardiniere. Open work handles. Very highest grade goods. Note low price.

Loy-Nel-Art 13 in. high, 6½ in. opening. Strictly High Grade Hand Decorated

No. 62 Umbrella Stand. Egyptian Design Around Top. 21 in. High 8½ in. Opening

No. 1109 Jardiniere and Pedestal. High Grade Mat Green

No. 202 Jardiniere. Latest design ever made. High Grade Mat Green

VERY HIGHEST GRADE POTTERY

The goods in the following assortments are strictly High Grade Hand Decorated and Beautifully modeled and shaded. Please do not confuse them with the cheap daubly imitation being offered at practically the same price. We believe these two assortments to be absolutely the BEST VALUE EVER OFFERED IN THESE POPULAR GOODS. PRICE MAKES THEM BIG SELLERS.

ASSORTMENT NO. 2 G. LOY-NEL-ART POTTERY contains:

4	only No. 205 Jardiniere	7½ in.	opening 9½ in.	across top doz.	$11.25	$3.75
3	"	8½	"	10½	"	15.00	3.75
2	"	9½	"	12	"	18.75	3.12
1	"	10½	"	13	"	22.50	1.88
1	1180	13 in. across top and Pedestal 18 in. high				5.85
1	62 Umbrella Stand 21 in. high 8½ in. opening					4.50
12	FINE PIECES LOY-NEL-ART POTTERY					Total $22.85

PRICE COMPLETE ASSORTMENT **$22.50**

ASSORTMENT No. 3F FINE MAT GREEN WARE contains:

4	only No. 202 Jardinieres	7 in.	opening 8 in.	across top doz.	$6.00	$2.00
3	"	8	"	9	"	8.00	2.00
2	"	10	"	11	"	12.00	2.00
2	"	13	"			18.00	1.50
1	1190	13 " across bulge and Pedestal 18 in. high				5.85
	72 Umbrella Stand 21 in. high 8½ in. opening					4.50
12	PIECES HIGH GRADE MAT GREEN WARE					Total $17.85

PRICE COMPLETE ASSORTMENT **$17.50**

11

No. 2030—Combination Jardiniere and Pedestal and Flower Pot

Our new Mat Green Glaze. A fine article.

30½ in. Jar, 10 in. Pedestal, each $3.25

No. 203

Combination Jardiniere and Flower Pot

Elegantly modeled and finished in Old Wheat Stone Green and the popular Mat Green. The inside pot is placed into the Jardiniere in the same finish as between Jardiniere. Bottom of pot is perforated and fresh from fire into which flowers pot. Will grow plants as well as any flower pot made. Its aid makes it in every way will appeal to every lover of decorative pottery.

No. 94—Plateaux

Here is an article which fills that essential "long felt want." It is decorative when used under a jardiniere or fern dish, or may be used as protection to table top under fed dishes, etc. Sells at sight. Finished in rich glazes.

8 in Blended colors .... per dozen $3.00

Combination Jardiniere and Flower Pot

5 inch Mat Green .... per dozen	$ 6.00
6½ inch Mat Green .... per dozen	9.00
7½ inch Mat Green .... per dozen	12.00
8½ inch Mat Green .... per dozen	18.00
9½ inch Mat Green .... per dozen	24.00
10½ inch Mat Green .... per dozen	36.00
5 inch Blended Glaze Colors .... per dozen	4.50
6½ inch Blended Glaze Colors .... per dozen	6.75
7½ inch Blended Glaze Colors .... per dozen	9.00
8½ inch Blended Glaze Colors .... per dozen	13.50
9½ inch Blended Glaze Colors .... per dozen	18.00
10½ inch Blended Glaze Colors .... per dozen	27.00

No. 2030—Combination Jardiniere and Pedestal and Flower Pot

Beautifully Blended Colors.

30½ in Jar, 10 in. Pedestal, each $3.00

No. 91—Combination Fern Dish and Liner

Two of these glazed in Mat Green like body of dish. Bottom of liner is perforated in ordinary flower pot and will grow ferns or plants equally as well. Especially designed for table and other interior decoration.

No. 91—Combination Fern Dish and Liner

Price includes both pieces.

4 inch Mat Green .... per dozen	$ 6.00
6 inch Mat Green .... per dozen	9.00
8 inch Mat Green .... per dozen	18.00

NEW HIGH GRADE MAT GREEN. EQUAL TO ANY MADE.

SHEET F.

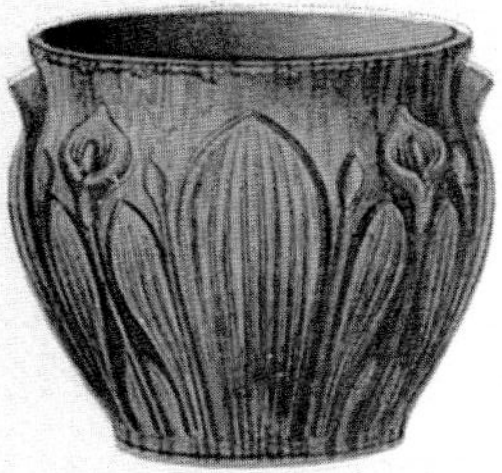

No. 202 Jardiniere
7½ in. Mat Green.....per dozen $ 6 00
8½ in. Mat Green.....per dozen 8 00
9½ in. Mat Green....per dozen 12 00
10½ in. Mat Green...per dozen 18 00
11½ in. Mat Green ..per dozen 30 00

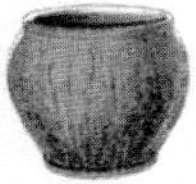

No. 115 Jardiniere
3½ inch Mat Green
Gross $30.00

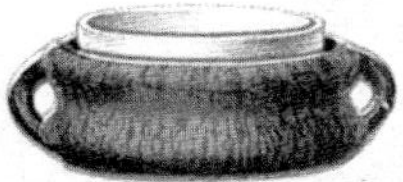

No. 90 Fern Dish
Fine Mat Green
4 in. with Liner ......dozen $ 4 00
6 in. with Liner.........dozen 8 00
8 in. with Liner.........dozen 12 00

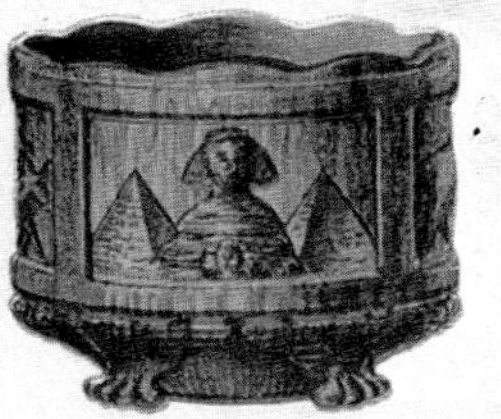

No 204 Egyptian Jardiniere
10½ in. Fine Mat Green, doz. $24 00

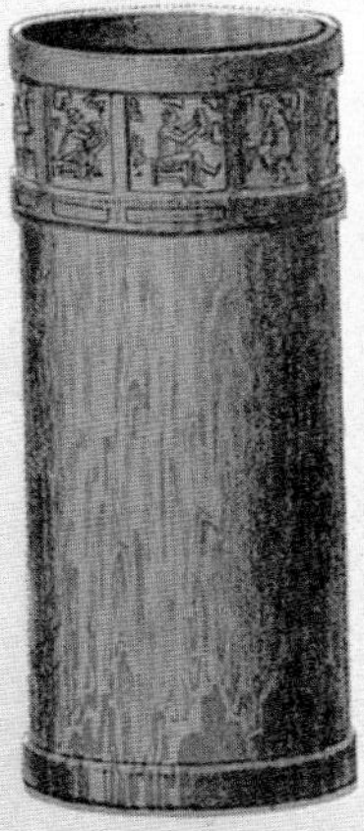

No. 72 Umbrella Stand
Egyptian Design Around Top
21 in. High 8½ in. Opening
High Grade Mat Green
Each $4.50

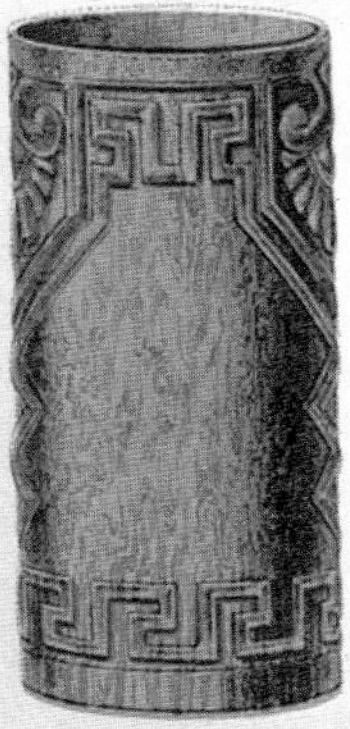

No. 60 Umbrella Stand
High Grade Mat Green
17 in. High 8 in. Opening
Each $3.00

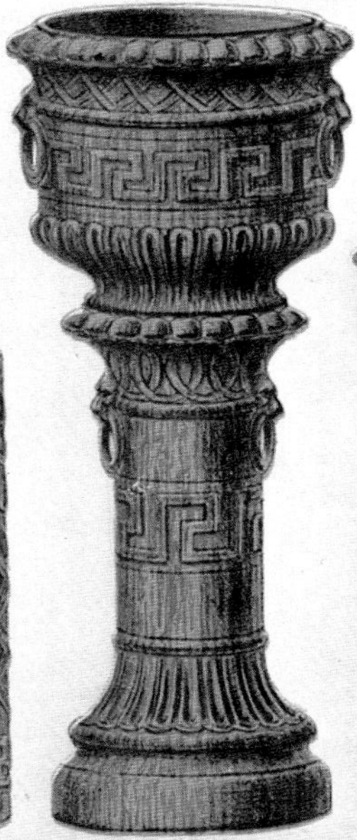

No. 1160 Jardiniere and Pedestal
Highest Grade Mat Green
Exceptionally Fine Design
12 in. Jar. 20 in. Pedestal, each $10.00
14 in. Jar. 23 in. Pedestal, each $20.00

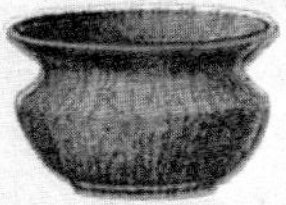

No. 1 Cuspidore
Mat Green
7 in. Nice Shape, doz. $5.00

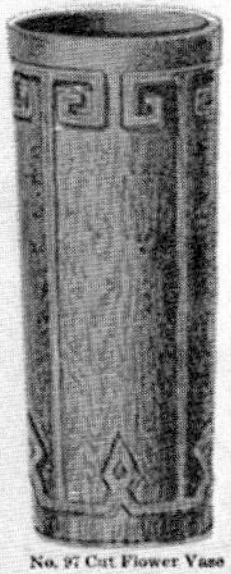

No. 97 Cut Flower Vase
Fine Mat Green
9 in. High.............. dozen $10 00
11 in. High ....dozen 15 00
13 in. High ....dozen 20 00
16 in. High..............dozen 30 00
21 in. High..............dozen 40 00

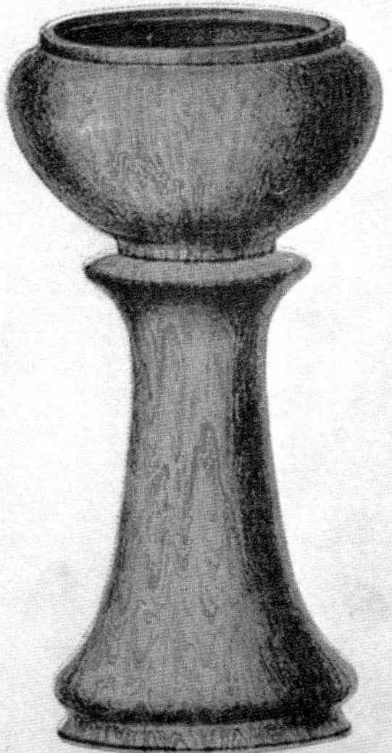

No. 1190 Jardiniere and Pedestal
High Grade Mat Green
12 in. Jar., 18 in. Pedestal, each $5.85

SUPPLEMENTARY SHEET K

No. 207—JARDINIERE
7½ inch Old Ivory.............per dozen $7.50

No. 208 JARDINIERE
8½ inch Old Ivory.............per dozen $12.50

No 2060—JARDINIERE AND PEDESTAL
Old Ivory.   Fine Modeling
11½ inch Jar, 18 inch Pedestal......each $ 7.50

No. 210—JARDINIERE
9½ inch Old Ivory.........per dozen $20.00

No. 209—JARDINIERE
10½ inch Old Ivory.........per dozen $30.00

No. 206—JARDINIERE
Old Ivory
11½ inch Jardiniere only........per dozen $40.50

Old Ivory Ware is our latest and probably our most popular product. Pieces are finely embossed and modeled---body in light cream, covered with smooth rich cream glaze. Modeling is brought out with rich brown in the incisions and around embossed work. It is extremely pleasing and harmonizes with any color scheme.

No. 46—CORN STEINS
Extra Size, 5½ inch high   per gross $40.50

No. 4746—CORN STEIN SET
Finished in Fine Glaze in Natural Colors. Consists of 1 Tankard and 6 Steins.
Price   ....per dozen sets $36.00

No. 47—CORN TANKARD
Extra Size, 12½ inch high...... per dozen $18.00

14

OLD IVORY WARE

SHEET F. F.

No. 79 Umbrella Stand
Old Ivory
21 in. high 10¾ in. opening
Doz. $72.00

No. 200—Jardiniere and Pedestal
Fine Blended Colors
11¾ in. Jard. 18 in. Pedestal Each $4.00
$7.50

No. 78 Umbrella Stand
Old Ivory
21 in. high 8¼ in. opening
Doz. $60.00

No. 210 Jardiniere
9½ in. Old Ivory $30.00

No. 207 Jardiniere
7½ in. Old Ivory Doz. $7.50

No. 209 Jardiniere
8¼ in. Old Ivory Doz. $12.50

No. 209 Jardiniere
10½ in. Old Ivory Doz. $30.00

15

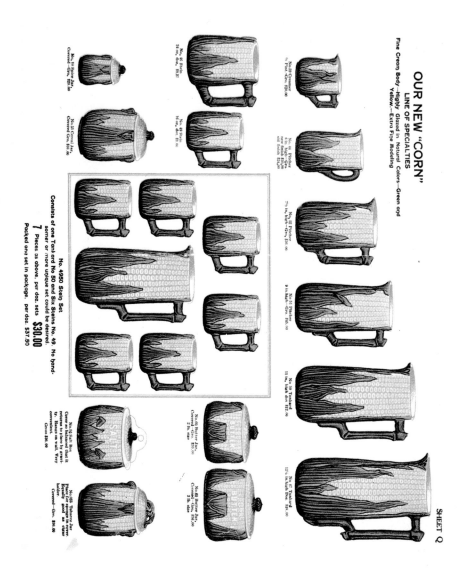

OUR NEW "CORN"

LINE OF SPECIALTIES

Fine Cream Body—Highly Glazed in Natural Colors—Green and
Yellow.—Extra Fine Modeling

SHEET Q

No. 46 Stein
24 oz., doz., $2.27

No. 49 Stein
16 oz., doz., $5.00

No. 59 Creamer
½ Pint. Gro., $20.00

No. 44 Pitcher
4 in. high—Gro.,
cover finish $20.00
old finish $24.00

No. 58 Spice Jar,
Covered—Gro., $20.00

No. 57 Cereal Jar,
Covered Gro. $26.00

No. 52 Pitcher
7½ in. high—Gro., $28.00

No. 51 Pitcher
9 in. high—Gro. $35.00

No. 50 Tankard
11 in. high doz. $12.00

No. 47 Tankard
12½ in. high Doz. $16.00

No. 4950 Stein Set

Consists of one Tan't and No 50 and Six Steins No. 49. No band.
somer or more unique set could be desired.

7 Pieces as above, per doz. sets $30.00

Packed one set in package. per doz. $37.50

No. 56 Salt Box
Cover so balanced that it
returns to place by grav-
ity. Hangs on wall. Very
convenient.
Gross $36.00

No. 61 Butter Jar,
Covered—Gro.,
2 lb. size

No. 60 Butter Jar,
Covered—Gro. $26.00
2 lb. size

No. 54 Salt Box
Covered—Gro., $20.00
2 lb. size

No. 45 Tobacco Jar
Place for sponge in cover
Equally good as either
holder
Covered—Gro. $36.00

16

STANDARD LEADER ASSORTMENT

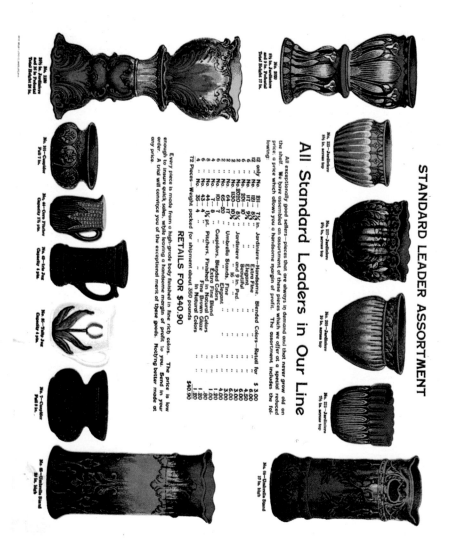

All Standard Leaders in Our Line

All exceptionally good sellers—pieces that are always in demand and that never grow old on the shelf. We have assembled an assortment of these pieces which we offer at a special reduced price—a price which allows you a handsome margin of profit. The assortment includes the following:

	No.			Retail for
12 only	No. 211	7½ in. Jardiniere—Handsome	Blended Colors	$3.00
12 "	No. 123	8½ " " Extra Fine		4.50
6 "	No. 117	9½ " " Elegant		6.00
6 "	No. 10	Beautiful		3.00
12 "	No. 2020 8½	Jardiniere on Ped.		3.00
12 "	No. 1130	Jardiniere and 9 in. Ped.		3.00
12 "	No. 64 17	16 "		4.00
6 "	No. 65 20	Umbrella Stands, Fine		3.00
2 "	No. 101 7	Cuspidors, Blended Elegant		4.00
6 "	No. 44	Extra Fine Blend		1.20
4 "	No. 7 8	Pitchers, Finished in Natural Colors		1.00
4 "	No. 43 1¾ pt.	Fine Brown Glaze		.80
6 "	No. 35 4	In Natural Colors		1.20
6 "	No. 4			.80
				.20
72 Pieces—Weight packed for shipment about 350 pounds				$40.90

RETAILS FOR $40.90

Every piece is made from a high-grade body finished in fine rich colors. The price is low enough to insure quick sales, while leaving a handsome margin of profit to you. Send in your order. A trial will convince you of the exceptional merit of these goods. Nothing better made at any price.

No. 120—Jardiniere 9½ in. Pedestal, Total Height 36 in.

No. 2020—Jardiniere 8½ in. across top

No. 123—Jardiniere 8½ in. across top

No. 117—Jardiniere 9½ in. across top

No. 201—Jardiniere 10 in. across top

No. 211—Jardiniere 7½ in. across top

No. 101—Cuspidor Full 7 in.

No. 44—Corn Pitcher Capacity 1¾ pts.

No. 43—6 in Jar Capacity 4 pts.

No. 35—Tulip Jar Capacity 4 pts.

No. 7—Cuspidor Full 8 in.

No. 64—Umbrella Stand 17 in. high

No. 65—Umbrella Stand 20 in. high

19

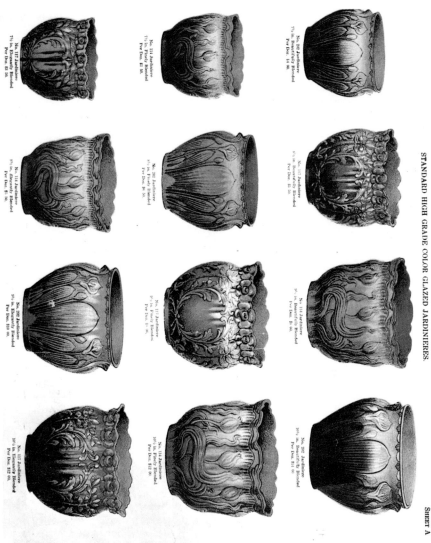

STANDARD HIGH GRADE COLOR GLAZED JARDINIERES.

SHEET A

21

HIGH GRADE FANCY COLOR GLAZED JARDINIERES.

SHEET B

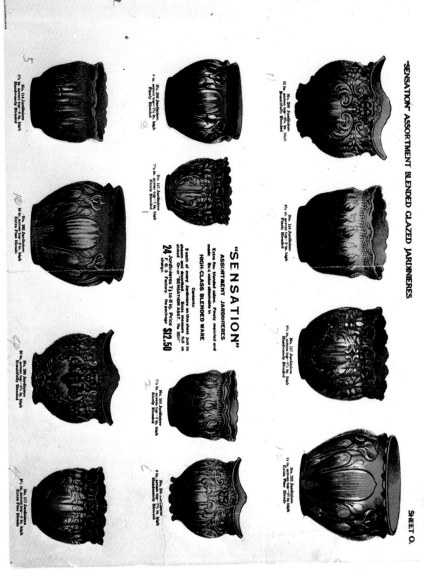

"SENSATION" ASSORTMENT BLENDED GLAZED JARDINIERES

SHEET O.

"SENSATION"

ASSORTMENT JARDINIERES

Extra fine blended color. Finely enameled and made. Be a value obtainable in

HIGH-CLASS BLENDED WARE

Contains:

1 each of every Jardiniere on this sheet just as shown. Every piece made as a value obtainable in "SENSATION ASST."

24 Jardinieres 7½ to 11 in. Price $12.50

F. O. B. Factory. No package charge.

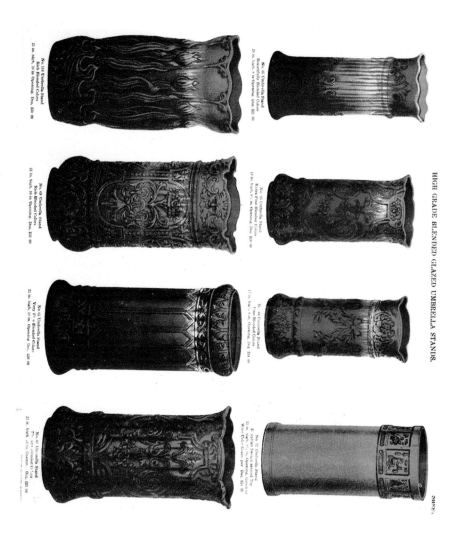

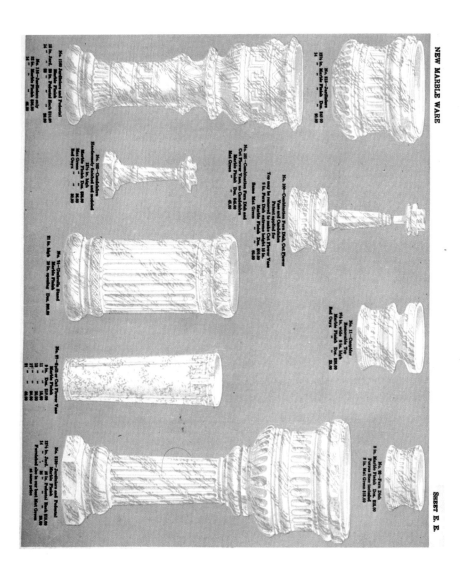

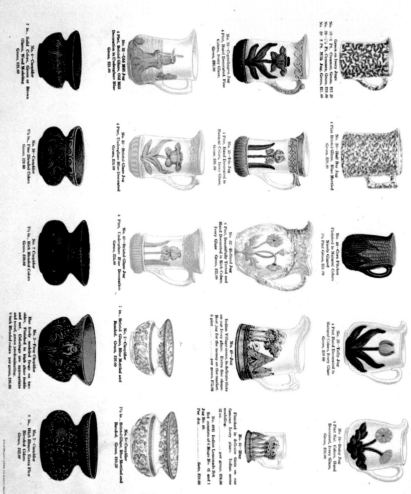

SHEET H.

26

OUR IVORY LINE---BEST UTILITY WARE IN THE WORLD

SHEET 1

High Glaze, Light Weight, Underglaze Decorations in Green

PINEAPPLE EMBOSSED GREEN-ON-IVORY MIXING BOWLS

6½ inch......per doz $4.60
5 inch......per doz .72
6 inch......per doz .84

7 inch......per doz $1.00   8 inch......per doz $1.20   9 inch......per doz $1.60

9 inch......per doz $2.00   9½ inch......per doz $2.40   10½ inch......per doz $2.80

11 inch......per doz $3.80

OUR FAMOUS GREEN-ON-IVORY SHOULDER NAPPIES

6 inch......per doz $0.84   7 inch......per doz $1.00   8 inch......per doz $1.40   9 inch......per doz $1.60   10 inch......per doz $2.00   11 inch......per doz $2.80

No. 15 COMBINET
Full Size, Fancy Shape
Green on Ivory Glaze......per dozen $12.00

"COREY" VASE
Finished in natural colors,
Green and Yellow
6 in. high, gross $21.00

"BILLY POSSUM" MONEY BANK
Finished in Green and
Brown Glaze
5½ in. high, gross $18.00

CUSTARD CUP
Green-on-Ivory
7 oz. green mottled, doz .50
10 oz. green mottled, doz .60

Covered Sanitary Refrigerator Bowl
Green-on-Ivory Finish
No. 10—6½ in. high, 5½ in. wide, doz $2.00
No. 11—5 in. high, 6½ in. wide, gross 5.00
No. 12—2½ in. high, 7½ in. wide, doz 4.00
All Refrigerator Bowls Covered.

27

Our Famous White and Decorated Bristol Glaze Ware

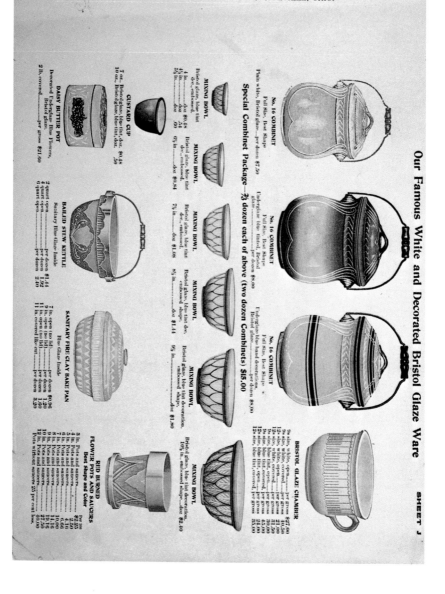

No. 16 COMBINET
Full Size, Best Shape
Plain white, Bristol glaze......per dozen $7.50

No. 16 COMBINET
Full Size, Best Shape
Underglaze blue tinted, Bristol
glaze......per dozen $8.00

No. 16 COMBINET
Full Size, Best Shape
Underglaze blue band decoration,
Bristol glaze......per dozen $9.00

Special Combinet Package—⅔ dozen each of above (two dozen Combinets) $15.00

MIXING BOWL.
Bristol glaze, blue tint
dec., embossed,
4 in.......doz $0.48
4½ in.......doz $0.54
5½ in.......60

MIXING BOWL.
Bristol glaze, blue tint
dec., embossed,
6½ in.......doz $0.84

MIXING BOWL.
Bristol glaze, blue tint
dec., embossed,
7½ in.......doz $1.08

MIXING BOWL.
Bristol glaze, blue tint dec.,
embossed shape,
8½ in.......doz $1.44

MIXING BOWL.
Bristol glaze, blue tint decoration,
embossed shape,
9½ in.......doz $1.80

MIXING BOWL.
Bristol glaze, blue tint decoration,
10½ in., embossed shape......doz $2.40

BRISTOL GLAZE CHAMBER
9s size, white, open......per gross $27.00
9s size, white, covered......per gross 40.50
12s size, white, open......per gross 21.00
12s size, white, covered......per gross 31.50
9s size, blue tint, open......per gross 30.00
9s size, blue tint, covered......per gross 45.00
12s size, blue tint, open......per gross 25.00
12s size, blue tint, covered......per gross 35.00

CUSTARD CUP
7 oz., Bristol glaze, blue tint, doz. $0.48
10 oz., Bristol glaze, blue tint, doz. .50

DAISY BUTTER POT
Decorated Underglaze Blue Flowers,
Bristol glaze,
2 lb., covered......per gross $21.00

BAILED STEW KETTLE
Sanitary Blue Glaze Inside
2 quart open......per doz $1.44
4 quart open......per doz 1.92
6 quart open......per doz 2.40

SANITARY FIRE CLAY BAKE PAN
Blue Glaze Inside
7 in., open (no lid)......per dozen $0.96
9 in., open (no lid)......per dozen 1.20
11 in., open (no lid)......per dozen 1.80
11 in., covered like cut......per dozen 3.20

RED BURNED FLOWER POTS AND SAUCERS
Best Shape and Color
	per 100
3 in., Pots and saucers	$2.25
4 in., Pots and saucers	2.50
5 in., Pots and saucers	4.10
6 in., Pots and saucers	4.66
7 in., Pots and saucers	6.65
8 in., Pots and saucers	10.00
9 in., Pots and saucers	11.16
10 in., Pots and saucers	15.15
11 in., Pots and saucers	27.50
12 in., Pots and saucers	40.00
Pots without saucers 25 per cent less	

NEW SPECIALS
Just Out
Send for Our
Special Sale Proposition

No. 202 Special Jardiniere

Especially good as a Dollar Leader.
6 inch Size, Blended Colors, fine Modeling. A "daisy". . . . . per gross $25.00

No. 75 Umbrella Stand

21 inch high, large opening, extra fine modeling. Old Independence. Hall on front, Liberty Bell on back, blended colors.
Per dozen $8.00

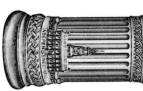

No. 2020, Jardiniere and Pedestal
New Special Size

8½ inch Jardiniere, 9 inch Pedestal.
Per dozen $15.00
Finely modeled and blended, excellent for a special.

No. 2060 Jardiniere and Pedestal
Green on Ivory Finish
Handsomely Modeled and Blended
11 in. Jardiniere, 18 in. Pedestal, each $4.00
Extra Good Value.

No. 45 Baby Mug

Two handles, so that baby can take hold with both hands. Handsomely finished, blue outside, cream inside. Big the seller.
Per gross $25.00

Covered Jug
Green on Ivory Finish
No. 28—1 pint. Per gross $33.00
No. 28—2 pint. Per gross $36.00

Covered Hall Boy
Green on Ivory Finish
4 Pint Size . . . . per gross $40.00

Covered Deep Dish
Blue Tint Decoration
5 inch Bristol Glaze . . per dozen $1.60
6 inch Bristol Glaze . . per dozen 1.80

Covered Deep Dish
Green on Ivory Finish
5 inch Size . . . . per dozen $1.60
6 inch Size . . . . per dozen 1.80
7 inch Size . . . . per dozen 2.10

29

BEST SELLING COMBINETS and CHAMBERS.

Note Assorted Packages

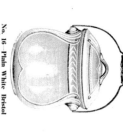

No. 15—Green-on-Ivory High Glaze Combinet
Fancy Shape, Extra Size, Covered and Baked
Per dozen $12.00
Here is the best low priced Combinet on the market today.

No. 16—Plain White Bristol Glaze Combinet
Covered and Baked
Full 9s size, per dozen $7.50

No. 16—Blue Tint Bristol Glaze Combinet
Covered and Baked
Full 9s size, per dozen $8.00

No. 16—Green Stippled Bristol Glaze Combinet
Covered and Baked
Full 9s size, per dozen $8.00

No. 16—Blue Band Bristol Glaze Combinet
Covered and Baked
Full 9s size, per dozen $8.00

Best Seller Asst. No. 1920

Contains: 2 dozen White Bristol Combinets, full size
½ dozen Blue Tint Bristol Combinets, full size
½ dozen Green Stipple Bristol Combinets, full size
½ dozen Blue Band Bristol Combinets, full size
4 dozen Green-on-Ivory Fancy Shape Combinets, extra large

One-Half Best Seller Assortment, No. 1935, Price $16.25

ASSORTMENT NO. 500
1 Dozen White and Dec. Combinets
(CONTENTS)
½ dozen No. 16 White Combinets
¼ dozen No. 16 Blue Band Combinets
¼ dozen No. 16 Blue Tint Combinets
1 Dozen Combinets, Price $7.50

ASSORTMENT NO. 960
2 Dozen White and Dec. Combinets
(CONTENTS)
1 dozen No. 16 White Combinets
½ dozen No. 16 Blue Band Combinets
½ dozen No. 16 Blue Tint Combinets
2 Dozen Combinets, Price $14.50

1 Dozen Popular Priced Combinets, Price only $32.00

ASSORTMENT NO. 1560
Combinets and Chambers
(CONTENTS)
1 dozen No. 16 White Combinets, full size
½ dozen No. 16 Blue Tint Combinets, full size
½ dozen No. 16 Green Stippled Combinets
3 dozen 9s. White Open Chambers
1 dozen 9s. White Covered Chambers
7 Dozen 12s White Open Chambers
7 Dozen Chambers and Combinets, Price $26.00

One-Half Asst. No. 1560, 3½ Dozen
Price $13.50

Bristol Glaze Chamber

9s. size, white, open per gross $25.00
9s. size, white, covered per gross 37.50
12s size, white, open per gross 20.00
12s size, white, covered per gross 30.00
9s. size, blue tint, open per gross 30.00
9s. size, blue tint, covered per gross 45.00
12s. size, blue tint, open per gross 24.00
12s. size, blue tint, covered per gross 35.00

ASSORTMENT NO. 675
Plain White Chambers
2½ dozen 9s. size, white, open Chambers
1 dozen 9s. size, white, covered Chambers
1 dozen 12s size, white, open Chambers
1 dozen 12s size, white, covered Chambers
5 Doz. Bristol Chambers, Price $11.25

No. 9—Jardiniere, 6½ in. Colored Glazes.

No. 31—Jug, 4 pt. Old Mill Decorated in Blue.

Ivory Mixing Bowl, 8 inch. Green Mottled Decoration.

Daisy Butter Jar. 2 lb. Blue Decoration. Fancy Embossed.

No. 36—Hall Boy Jug. 4 pint. Blue Mottled. Bristol Glaze.

No. 44—Cream Pitcher, 1½ pint. Corn Decorated in Natural Colors.

No. 5—Cuspidor, 7½ in. Blue Mottled and Banded.

No. 4—Cuspidor. 7 in. Fancy Glazed.

WONDER ASSORTMENT No. 1080.

1 dozen No. 9—6½ inch Fine Color Glazed Jardinieres.
1 " No. 31—4 pt. Old Mill Blue Decorated Bristol Jugs.
1 " No. 44—1½ pt. Fancy Corn Decorated Cream Pitcher.
1 " No. 4—7 in. Fancy Color Glazed Cuspidors.
1 " No. 8—8 in. Fancy Green on Ivory Mixing Bowls.
1 " No. 8½ in. Fancy Blue Tinted Bristol Mixing Bowl.
1 " No. 2—Sanitary Lid Daisy Butter Jars.
1 " No. 2 qt. Fire Clay Baked Preserving Kettles.
1 " No. 9 in. Fire Clay Sanitary Baking Dishes.
1 " No. 36—4 pt. Blue Mottled Hall Boy Jugs.
1 " No. 5—7½ in. Blue Mottled and Banded Cuspidors.
1 " No. 01—Fancy Corn Vase or Spoon Holder.

12 dozen Big Fast Selling 10c, 15c and 20c items.

Price._____

Above can be sold at a popular price and net a handsome profit. Each item a leader of its class.

Corn Vase or Spoon Holder. Decorated in Natural Colors.

Preserving Kettle. 2 qt. Fire Clay. Wood Lift Bail.

Baking Dish. 9 in. Fire Clay. Sanitary Non-crazing Glaze.

Bristol Mixing Bowl. 8½ in. Blue Tinted.

31

Stoneware Jugs
Black Glaze Top and White Bottom. Best Shoulder Jug on the market.
½ Gal. Handled, per 100 $ 11.65
1 " " " 100 $ 17.50
2 " " " 100 $ 35.00

Stoneman Butter Jars
Extra Fine Quality, Bristol Glaze Goods.
½ Gal. Low Shape, per 100 $ 9.15
1 " High " 100 $ 13.15
2 " " " 100 $ 27.50
Big Sellers Everywhere.

Stew or Preserve Kettle
2 qt. Bailed, very best. Doz. $1.44
4 qt. " " " " 1.92

Baking Pan
7 in., Extra Fine. Doz. $1.60
9 in. " " " 1.80

Bread Jar
Here is an article which will certainly fill "a long felt want." Big seller because very useful. Best in Blue as illustrated. Per Doz. $6.00

Every Article is made with best Bristol Sanitary Non-Crazing Glaze.

Tankard Jug
9 in., 5 pint Blue Dec. Gro. $25.00

Blue Mottled Mixing Bowls
8 in. Extra Deep Shape, Doz. $1.44
9 in. " " " 1.80
10 in. " " " 2.40

Blue Lined Shoulder Bowls
6 in. Extra Deep Shape, Doz. $.84
7 in. " " " 1.08
8 in. " " " 1.44

Stirring Bowls
1 quart, Decorated, Doz. $ .90
2 quart " " 1.20
4 quart " " 1.80

Hanging Salt Box
Blue Dec. Hinged Wood Cover, best made, Gro. $20

Indian Butter
Embossed Indian Scene
3 lb. Covered, Gro. $21.00
2 lb. Uncovered, " 12.50

Holland Butter
Dutch Kids in Blue
5 lb. Covered, Gro. $24.00
5 lb. Uncovered, " 15.00

Custard Cup
10 oz. Blue Dec. Gro. $6.00

Combinet
Full Sized, Covered and Bailed, doz. $7.50

Chamber
9s White Open, Gross $25.00
12s White Open, Gross 29.00
Covers one-half Price of Chamber

Cuspidor
Full 7½ in. Blue Mottled and Handled, Self-righting Shape, Best Made, Gross $19.20

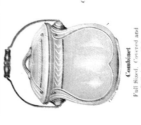

Rolling Pin—15 in., Blue Dec., Polished Handle, Gro. $24.00

BOOK OF ILLUSTRATIONS
AND PRICES OF GOODS

MANUFACTURED BY THE

BRUSH-McCOY POTTERY CO.

PRINCIPAL OFFICE AT

Zanesville, Ohio, U. S. A.

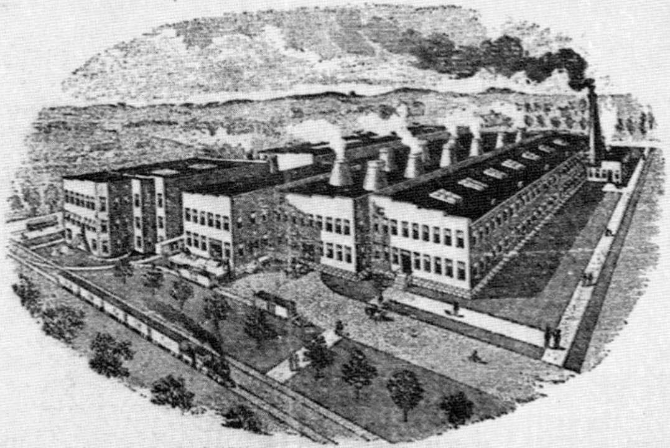

PLANT No. 1, ZANESVILLE, OHIO

PLANT No. 2, ROSEVILLE, OHIO

COMPLETE Lines of Art and Glazed Jardinieres, Pedestals, Umbrella Stands, Cuspidors, etc. Our famous "Green-on-Ivory" Utility Ware. Our New "Whitestone" and "Flemish Blue" Specialties. High Grade Stoneware, Flower Pots and Cooking Ware.

33

GRAPE WARE—High Glaze and Natural Colors. Best line of Utility Articles on the Market.

CORN WARE—Finished in high glaze in natural colors.

34

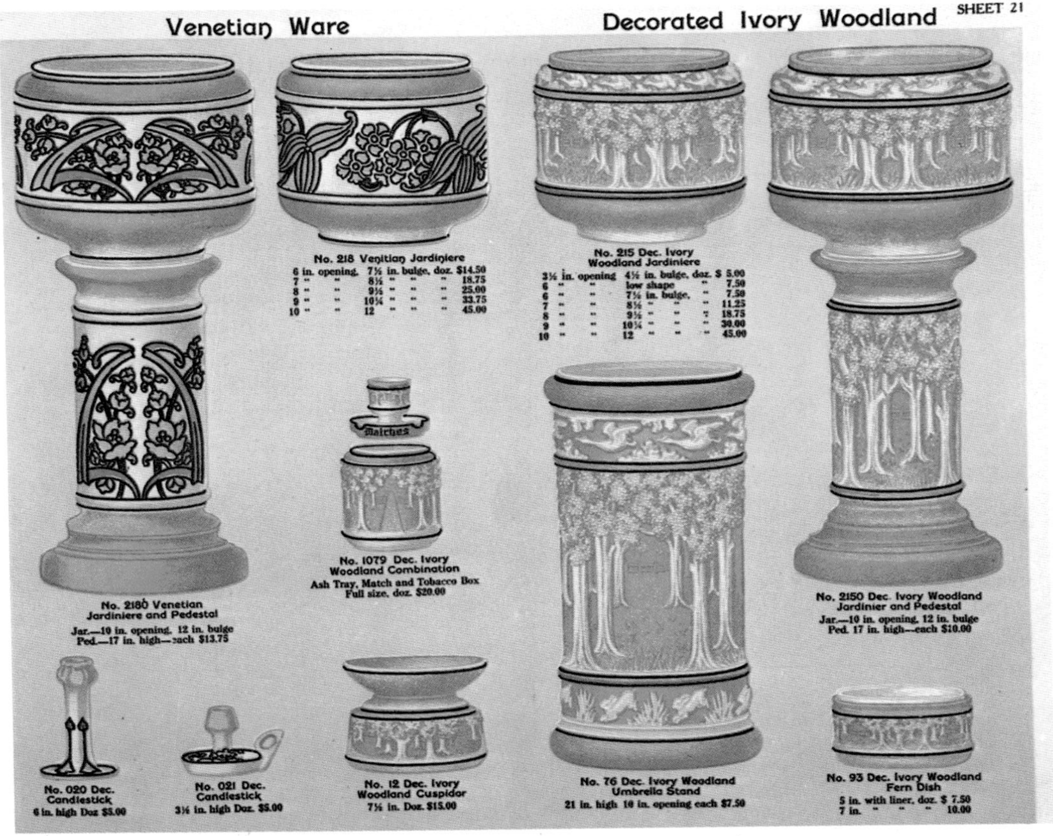

No. 2150 Dec. Ivory Woodland
Jardinier and Pedestal
Jar—10 in. opening, 12 in. bulge
Ped. 17 in. high—each $10.00

No. 93 Dec. Ivory Woodland
Fern Dish
5 in. with liner, doz. $ 7.50
7 in. " " — " 10.00

No. 215 Dec. Ivory Woodland Jardiniere

3½ in. opening	4½ in. bulge, doz.	$ 5.00
6 " "	6½ " "	7.50
6½ " "	low shape	7.50
7 " "	7¼ in. bulge	9.00
8 " "	8½ " "	11.25
9 " "	9½ " "	15.75
9½ " "	10¾ " "	28.00
10 " "	12 " "	43.00

No. 76 Dec. Ivory Woodland
Umbrella Stand
21 in. high 10 in. opening each $7.50

No. 215 Venetian Jardiniere

6 in. opening	7½ in. bulge, doz.	$14.50
7 " "	8½ " "	18.75
8 " "	9½ " "	25.00
9 " "	10¾ " "	33.75
10 " "	12 " "	43.00

No. 1079 Dec. Ivory
Woodland Combination
Ash Tray, Match and Tobacco Box
Full size, doz. $20.00

No. 12 Dec. Ivory
Woodland Cuspidor
7½ in. Doz. $15.00

No. 2150 Venetian
Jardiniere and Pedestal
Jar—10 in. opening, 12 in. bulge
Ped.—17 in. high—each $13.75

No. 021 Dec.
Candlestick
3½ in. high Doz. $3.00

No. 020 Dec.
Candlestick
6 in. high Doz $3.00

No. 91 Oriental Fern Dish
7 in. with liner doz. $11.25
8 " " " " 16.00
9 " " " " 22.50

No. 221 Oriental
only—doz.
7 in. Jardiniere
8 " "
9 " "
10 " "
11 " "
12 " "
13 " "
14 " "

$15.00
22.50
30.00
45.00
65.00
105.00

No. 2216 Oriental Jardiniere and Pedestal
12 in. Jardiniere | Price complete $52.50
18 " Pedestal |

No. 76 Green Woodland Umbrella Stand
21 in. high .... Each $6.00
19 in. opening } Each $4.50

STRICTLY HIGH GRADE ASSORTMENTS

Both of these wares are exceptional value and these assortments are just right for samples.

No. 67 Oriental Umbrella Stand
21 in. high—each $12.00

ASSORTMENT No. 1313 GREEN WOODLAND Contains

			Doz.	Each
2 only No.	215 Jard. 7 in. opening 8½ in. bulge		$7.50	$1.25
2 " "	8 " " 9½ "	12.50	2.08
1 " "	9 " " 10½ "	20.00	1.67
1 " "	10 " " 12 "	30.00	2.50
1 " "	2150 Jard. 10 in. Pedestal 17 in. high each		6.00
1 " "	76 Umbrella Stand, 21 in. high each		4.50

Total $18.00

8 FINE PIECES GREEN WOODLAND POTTERY. PRICE COMPLETE ASSORTMENT $17.50

ASSORTMENT No. 1413 ORIENTAL WARE Contains

		Doz.	Each
1 only No. 221 7 in. Jardiniere—extra large		$15.00	$1.25
1 " " " 8 " "	22.50	1.88
1 " " " 9 " "	30.00	2.50
1 " " " 10 " "	45.00	3.75
1 " " 2230 10 in. Jardiniere, 18 in. Ped. each		12.50
1 " " 67 23 in. Umbrella Stand, each		12.50

Total $34.38

6 FINE PIECES ORIENTAL POTTERY, COMPLETE ASSORTMENT, PRICE $33.75

No. 91 Green Woodland Fern Dish
7 in. with Liner Doz. $9.15
7 " " " 11.00

No. 215 Green Woodland
opening 8½ in. bulge Doz.
4 in. 9½ " $4.90
7 " 10½ " 7.50
8 " 12 " 12.00
9 " 20.00
10 " 30.00

No. 2230 Green Woodland Jardiniere and Pedestal
Jar. 10 in. Opening, 8 in. Ruler
Ped. 17 in. high—Each $9.00

HIGH GRADE BLENDED WARE. Nothing Better Made.

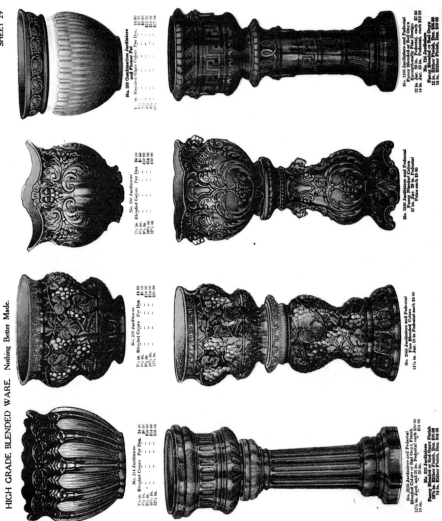

"RADURO BLENDED WARE"

No. 201 Jardiniere
Blended Colors
7½ in. ... $3.50
8½ in. ... $5.50
9½ in. ... $8.50
10½ in. ... $12.00

No. 202 Jardiniere
Newly Blended Per Gro. $24.00
Elegantly M'f'd Per Doz.
6½ in. ... $4.00
7½ in. ... $6.00
8½ in. ... $8.50
9½ in. ... $12.00
10½ in. ... $18.00
11½ in. ... $24.00

No. 114 Jardiniere
Blended Colors Per Doz.
7½ in. ... $3.50
8½ in. ... $6.00
9½ in. ... $9.00
10½ in. ... $12.00
12 in. ... $24.00

No. 117 Jardiniere
Blended Colors Per Doz.
7½ in. ... $3.50
8½ in. ... $5.50
9½ in. ... $8.00
10½ in. ... $12.00
12 in. ... $18.00

No. 251 Jardiniere
7½ in. screen top Gro. $60.00

No. 359 Jardiniere
4½ in. Blended Gro. $10.00
5½ in. Blended Gro. ....

No. 212 Jardiniere
Blended 7 in. Gro. $24.00

No. 2920 Jardiniere and Pedestal
Ex. Fine Modeling Finest M'f'd Colors
14 in. Jar. 77 in. Pedestal each $4.00

No. 50 Umbrella Stand
Blended 26 in. Chrome. Doz. $72.00

No. 64 Umbrella Stand
Fine Blended Colors
17 in. high, 9 in. Chrome. Doz. $14.00

No. 1175 Jardiniere and Pedestal
Fine Blended Colors
7½ in. Jar. 7 in. Pedestal each $6.00
12 in. Jar. ½ in. Pedestal each $6.00

No. 2910 Jardiniere and Pedestal
Richly Blended Colors
12½ in. Jar. 20 in. Pedestal each $7.00

NEW NAVARRE FAIENCE

SILKEN MAT GREEN

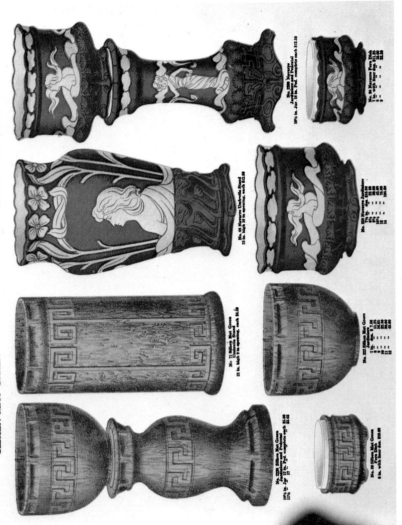

Cobalt Blue--High Gloss Glaze. Rich Gold Decoration

No. 202½. Half Boy Jug.
Deep Cobalt Blue.
Gold edge—Gold.
Fleur-de-lis.
4 pint, dozen..........$4.50

No. 103 Cut Soap Slab.
Dark Blue.
Rich Glaze.
4½ in. di...
Green..........$20.00

No. 127. Cuspidor.
Deep Cobalt Blue Glaze.
Gold decoration as shown.
9½ in. extra high, doz..$4.50

FOR BABY--Entirely New
Rich Blue and Gold Finish.

No. 450.
Two Handled Baby Mug.
Blue and Gold.
Gross..$20.00

No. 477 B.
Overhanging Edge Baby Bowl.
Blue and Gold.
Gross....$20.00

No. 329
Blue and Gold Baby Pitcher.
Gross....$20.00

We will furnish any of the above stamped with Adv. in gold for cost of stamp and 10 per cent. additional cost.

No. 675D. Baby Plate
Blue and Gold.
7½ inch. Gross......$52.50

Our Famous Green-on-Ivory Ware—Nothing Better at the Price.

No. 36. Half Boy Jug.
Green-on-Ivory Finish.
4-Pint..........gross $20.00

Green on Ivory Jugs.
No. 37 1 Pt. Creamer, gro. $12.20
No. 28—1 Pt. Cream. gro. $18.00
No. 29—3 Pt. Milk Jug. gro. $21.60

No. 8 Cream Jug.
Pours from side.
1 Pint. Green on Ivory
Finish.
Per gross, $13.80.

No. 137. Custard Cup.
Green on Ivory.
7-oz. green mod. doz. $ .60
10-oz. Green mod., doz. .72

No. 104. Soap Slab
Sea Green Glaze.
4½ in. in diam. gro. $20.00

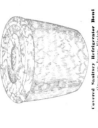

Covered Sanitary Refrigerator Bowl
Green on Ivory Finish.
No. 110. 4½ in. high, 5¼ in. wide, doz. $2.00
No. 111. 5½ in. high, 6¼ in. wide, doz. 2.40
No. 112. 5 in. high, 7¼ in. wide, doz. 4.00
All Refrigerator Bowls Covered.

No. 125. Shoulder Napples
Famous Green on Ivory Finish.
6 in. Baking Dish shape, doz. $ .84
7 in. Baking Dish shape, doz. 1.00
8 in. Baking Dish shape, doz. 1.10
9 in. Baking Dish shape, doz. 2.00
10 in. Baking Dish shape, doz. 2.40
11 in. Baking Dish shape, doz. 3.00

No. 124 Mixing Bowls.
Famous Green on Ivory Finish.
4½ inch embossed shape, doz. $ .60
6 inch embossed shape, doz. .72
7 inch embossed shape, doz. .84
8 inch embossed shape, doz. 1.00
9 inch embossed shape, doz. 1.60
10 inch embossed shape, doz. 2.00
11 inch embossed shape, doz. 3.00
12 inch embossed shape, doz. 4.00
14 inch embossed shape, doz. 9.00

No. 15. Combinet
Full Size. Fancy Shape.
Green on Ivory Glaze, per doz., $12.00.

40

Mitusa

No. 039 Cleo Vase
9½ in. high, doz. $12.60

No. 037 Cleo Vase
9½ in. high, doz. $14.20

No. 041 Cleo Vase
11 in. high, doz. $18.00

No. 040 Cleo Vase
12 in. high, doz. $21.40

No. 043 Cleo Vase
11 in. high, doz. $21.40

No. 042 Cleo Vase
11½ in. high, doz. $24.00

No. 97—Aegean Vase
9 in. doz. $23.50
11 ″ ″ 30.00
13 ″ ″ 54.00
17 ″ ″ 72.00
21 ″ ″ 100.00

No. 97-Leynel Art Vase
9 in. doz. $22.00
11 ″ ″ 18.00
13 ″ ″ 24.00
17 ″ ″ 36.00
21 ″ ″ 45.00

No. 97
Mat Green Vase
9 in. doz. $12.00
11 ″ ″ 18.00
13 ″ ″ 24.00
17 ″ ″ 36.00
21 ″ ″ 45.00

CLEO VASES GROUP NO. 3615—2 dozen (4 each above) only $36.00 List.

"Cleo" and Blue Bird Vases are Ivory Glaze—Handsomely decorated as shown.

Fancy Glazed Candlesticks

No. 044 B. Vase
11 in. high,
doz. $10.80

No. 037 B. Vase
9½ in. high,
doz. $8.25

No. 041 B. Vase
11 in. high,
doz. $9.00

No. 040 B. Vase
12 in. high,
doz. $10.80

No. 043 B. Vase
11 in. high,
doz. $10.80

No. 042 B. Vase
11½ in. high,
doz. $12.00

No. 029 P
4-inch

No. 027 P
5½-inch

No. 029 P
4-inch

No. 029 E
6-inch

Finished in fancy blended glazes, fine designs—extra good
cup for candles. Either number or assorted, per gross $32.40

BLUE BIRD GROUP NO. 3715—2 doz. (4 each above) only $18.00

No. 88
Azalea or High Fern
Jardiniere--Blended Colors
4 in. with liner doz. $ 3.60
6 ″ ″ 7.20
8 ″ ″ 12.00

No. 89—Fern Dish
Mat Green
8 in. with Liner Doz. $12.00

No. 90—Fern Dish
Log-Nel Art
4 in. with Liner, Doz. $6.00
6 ″ 12.00
8 ″ 18.00

No. 95—Dec. Ivory Fern
and Liner
6 in. doz. $9.00 7 in. doz. $12.00

No. 39—AEgean Inlaid Fern
with liner 8 in. doz. 18.00

No. 94 Navarre Fern Dish
7 in. with liner doz. $18.00
8 ″ ″ 24.00

SAMPLE FERN DISH GROUP NO. 3815—1 each of all sizes and styles shown
above—12 assorted—only **$12.00 List.**

No. 060—Frog

No. 061—Turtle

No. 062—Duck

No. 063—Fish

No. 451—Jap. Tray for Miniature Gardens
9 inches Brown or Green   doz. $ 9.00
12 ″ ″ 13.50
14 ″ ″ 22.50

No. 1079
Brown Woodland
Tobacco Box
Comb. top, doz. $6.00

No. 605
Corn Tobacco Box
Doz. $3.00

Submerged Cut Flower Holders--Latest Novelties--Fine Glazed
Colors--any one or assorted, doz. **$4.50**

BRIGHTON GROUP NO. 3815 DECORATED IVORY NOVELTIES--1 Gross $30.00 List

No. 45—Two Handled
Baby Mug

No. 077—Wide Bottom
Baby Bowl

No. 57—Baby Pitcher

No. 072—Post Card
Holder

No. 215—4 inches
Woodland Jardiniere

No. 90—3 inches
Fern Dish

No. 132—1 Pint
Pitcher

No. 229—3 inches
B. B. Jardiniere

BRIGHTON IVORY DECORATED WARE--Extra Value in Quick Selling Novelties

No. 029—P-6 inches
Candlestick

No. 134—Ash Tray
and Match Holder

BRIGHTON
GROUP
NO.
3915

Dozen	No. 45	Baby Mug
1	077	Bowl
1	57	Pitcher
1	072	Post Card Holder
1	215—4 inch	Jardiniere
1	90—3 inch	Fern Dish
1	132—1 Pt.	Pitcher
1	229 3 inch	Jardiniere
1	029 P 6 inch	Candlestick
1	134	Ash Tray
1	100	Soap Dish
1	027 P 5½ inch	Candlestick

Price for 12
dozen. Group
No. 3915

$30.00 LIST

No. 100—Blue Bird
Soap or Pin Tray

No. 027 P—5½ inches
Candlestick

41

ROMAN DECORATED POTTERY

ASST. No. 2414---I each of the 5 Roman
Jardinieres below---list $12.00

No. 218—Roman Dec. Jar
6 in. opening, 7½ in. bulge
Doz. $15.00

No. 219—Roman Dec. Jar
7 in. opening, 8½ in. bulge
Doz. $18.00

No. 216—Roman Dec. Jar
8 in. opening, 9½ in. bulge
Doz. $24.00

No. 219—Roman Dec. Jar
9 in. opening, 10½ id. bulge
Doz. $36.00

No. 218—Roman Dec. Jar
10 in. opening, 12 in. bulge
Doz. $54.00

FLORA Dec. Jardinieres and Pedestals

ASST. No. 2514---I each of the 5 Flora
Jardinieres below---list $13.50

No. 219—Flora
6 in. open, 7½ in. bulge,
Color—Canary, Doz. $17.50

No. 218—Flora
7 in. open, 8½ in. bulge, Doz. $22.50
Color—Salmon

No. 216—Flora
8 in. open, 9½ in. bulge, Doz. $30.00
Color—Umber

No. 218—Flora
9 in. open, 10½ in. bulge, Doz. $40.50
Color—Maroon

No. 218—Flora
10 in. open, 12 in. bulge, Doz. $54.00
Color—Sea Green

No. 2180---FLORA JAR and PED. (Style of No. 2150 Woodland shown on Page 60) 10 in. Jar. 17 in. Ped., Each $16.50

VENITIAN DECORATED POTTERY

ASST No. 2614---I each of the 5 Venitian
Jardinieres below---list $13.50

No. 219—Venitian
6 in. opening, 7½ in. bulge
Dozen $17.40

No. 219—Venitian
7 in. opening, 8½ in. bulge
Dozen $22.50

No. 216—Venitian
8 in. opening, 9½ in. bulge
Dozen $30.00

No. 218—Venitian
9 in. opening, 10½ in. bulge
Dozen $40.50

No. 218—Venitian
10 in. opening, 12 in. bulge
Dozen $54.00

No. 2180---VENITIAN JAR and PED. (Style of No. 2150 Woodland shown on Page 60) 10 in. Jar. 17 in. Ped., Each $16.50

Beautirose Ware

No. 117—Jardiniere

7½ inch Beautirose, Dozen	$12.00
8½ " " "	15.00
9½ " " "	22.50
10½ " " "	33.00
12 " " "	45.00

Beautirose Asst. No. 2714
CONTENTS:
1 each, 7½, 8½, 9½, 10½ inch
Jardinieres
1 only, each size Jar and Ped.
6 Pcs. Beautirose, list $17.25

Dresden Asst. No. 2814
CONTENTS:
1 each, , 8½, 9½, 10½ Jars.
1 No. 6 umbrella Jar.
1 Jar. a ed.
1 each 4, 6, and 8 Fern Dishes.
9 Pieces Dresden, list $27.00

Dresden Dec. Ware

No. 228—Jardiniere

7½ inch Dresden, Dozen,	$13.50
8½ " " "	18.00
9½ " " "	27.00
10½ " " "	42.00

No.—Beautirose Jar. and Ped.
12 in. Jar. 17 in. Ped. each $9.00

No. 1170—Beautirose
Jardiniere and Pedestal
7½ in. Jard. 7 in. Ped.
Each $6.00

No. 90—Dresden Fern
4 in. with liner Doz. $6.00
4 " " 12.00
5 " " 22.50

No. 62—Dresden Umbrella Jar
22 in. high. Each $4.00

No. 2280—Dresden Jard. and Ped.
Jard. 10 in. opening. 12 in. bulge.
Ped. 19 in. Each $10.00

42

NEW MARBLE AND "IVOTINT" WARE

No. 2190 Jard. and Pedestal
Decorated Autumn Oak Leaf
12 in. Jard. 20 inch Ped. Complete $12.00

No. 74—Umbrella Jard. Marble
21 in. high, 10 in. opening
doz. $72.00

No. 1100—Marble Jard. and Ped.
12 in. Jard. 20 in. Ped. each, $12.00
14   25   24.00
No. 116—Marble Jardiniere
12 in. Jards. only. doz. $43.50
14   57.00

No. 2130 Marble Jard. and Ped
12½ in. Jard. 26 in. Ped, each, $18.00
14   26   24.00
No. 213—Marble Jardiniere
12½ in. Jards. only. doz. $57.60
14   108.00

"Ivotint" Basket Ware

No. 96 Vase
9 in. high, doz. $18.00
12 in. high, doz. $6.00

No. 451 Hanging Fern
Ivotint Basket
8½ in. with liner, doz. $27.00

Sample Group No. 2515
Ivotint Basket Ware
1 only No. 220 Jardiniere 6 inch
1   "   "   "   7 inch
1   "   "   "   8   "
1   "   "   "   9   "
1   "   "   "   10   "
1   "   2000 Jard. & Pedestal
1   "   402 Umbrella Stand
7 Pcs Ivotint Basket Ware $26.00 List

No. 220 Jardiniere
Ivotint Basket
6 in.   dozen $6.00
7   "   9.00
8   "   13.00
9   "   24.00
10   "   26.00
11   "   34.00
12   "   30.00

No. 2000 Jardiniere and Pedestal
Ivotint Basket
Jardiniere 11 inch   Pedestal 17 inch
Total height 27 inch.   Complete each $10.00
Jardiniere 13 inch.   Pedestal 20 inch.
Total height 21 inch—each $15.00

No. 452 Window Box—Ivotint Basket
12 in. long 6 in. wide with liner doz. $60.00

No. 402 Umbrella Stand
Ivotint Basket
21 in. high. each $9.00

Extra Values in Handsome Umbrella Stands

No. 64—Umbrella Jar
17 in. high. Doz. $18.00

No. 75—Umbrella Jar
21 in. high. Doz. $36.00

No. 74—Umbrella Jar
22 in. high. Doz. $45.00

No. 402H—Umbrella Stand
Blended Basket
20½ in. high. Doz. $45.00

No. 76—Green Woodland Umbrella Jar
21 in. high. 10 in. opening. each $5.40

No. 71—Umbrella Jar Moss Green
21 in. high. each $3.75
No. 82—Umbrella Jar Moss Green
Same design as No. 71 Jar
19 in. high. each $2.76

No. 62—Umbrella Jar Loynel Art
21 in. high. 9 in. opening.
Price each. $6.00
No. 60—Umbrella Jar Loynel Art
17 in. high. 8 in. opening
Price each. $4.50

No. 71—Umbrella Stand
21 in. Aegean Inlaid
each $12.00

No. 75—Umbrella Stand
21 in. Bon-Ton. Each $6.00

No. 74—Umbrella Jard. Marble
22 in. high. 10 in. opening.
Doz. $72.00

Novelty Grass Growing Hobo Head and Pig

Plant seed on them
fill with water and watch
them grow.

No. 070 Grass Growing Hobo, gross $21.60
No. 079 Grass Growing Pig, gross 21.60
Package of Special Seed with each

No. 076
Grass Growing
Head

No. 079—Grass Pig

No. 039 Cleo Vase
9½ in. high doz. $12.00

No. 044 Cleo. Vase
11 in. high doz. $18.00

No. 042 Cleo Vase
11 in. high doz. $21.00

No. 042 Cleo Vase
11½ in. high doz. $24.00

No. 97—Aegean Vase
9 in. deg. $21.00
11 " 30.00
13 " $4.00

Fancy Glazed Money Banks

No. 069
Hobo Money
Bank

No. 080—Pig Bank

No. 068
Frog Bank

No. 069 Hobo Money Bank, gross $21.60
No. 080 Pig Money Bank, gross 21.60
No. 068 Frog Money Bank, gross 14.40

CLEO VASES GROUP No. 1216—2 dozen (6 each above) only $36.00

No. 050—Frog

No. 061—Turtle

No. 062—Duck

No. 063—Fish

**Submerged Cut Flower Holders--Latest Novelties--Fine Glazed
Colors--any one or assorted. Doz. $4.50**

No. 451H—Hanging Fern
Basket—Blended
8½ in. with liner. Doz. $18.00

44

The Brush-McCoy Pottery Co. [Z]anesville, Ohio., U. S. A.

M-Ausa TRADE MARK

CATALOGUE NO. 16 | SHEET 16A

"Sylvan" and "Bon-Ton" Tinted Ivory Glazed Ware—HIGH GRADE LIGHT COLORED MEDIUM PRICED.

This ware is finely finished-elegantly colored and glazed and will compare favorably with ivory ware formerly sold at three to four times the price.

No. 233—3½ in., doz., $2.25
No. 233—4½ in., doz. 2.70

No. 233—Sylvan 5¼ in. across top Doz., $3.60 · No. 206—Bon-Ton 6½ in across top Doz., $3.60 · No. 214—Bon-Ton 6½ in. across top Doz., $3.60 · No. 233—Sylvan 6½ in. across top Doz., $6.00

Group No. 2216 New Tinted Jardinieres

GROUP No. 2216 Contains:
- 1 doz. No. 233—5¼ in. Sylvan Jard.
- 2 " " 206—6½ in. Bon-Ton Jard.
- 2 " " 214—6½ in. Bon-Ton. Jard.
- 1 " " 233—6½ in. Sylvan Jard.

PRICE FOR 6 doz. $24.00 List

ONE-HALF GROUP NO. 2216 (3 doz.) $12.00 LIST

No. 214—Bon-Ton 7½ in. across top Doz., $7.20 · No. 233—Sylvan 7½ in. across top Doz., $9.00 · No. 206—Bon-Ton 7½ in. across top Doz., $7.20

Group No. 2316 New Tinted Jardinieres

GROUP No. 2316 Contains:
- 1⅓ doz. No. 214, 7½ in. Bon-Ton Jard.
- 1⅓ " " 233, 7½ in. Sylvan Jard.
- 1⅓ " " 206, 7½ in. Bon-Ton Jard.

PRICE FOR 4 doz. $30.00 List

ONE-HALF GROUP NO. 2316 (2 doz.) $15.00 LIST

No. 206—Bon-Ton 8½ in. across top Doz., $12.00 · No. 233—Sylvan 8½ in. across top Doz., $15.00 · No. 214—Bon-Ton 8½ in. across top Doz., $12.00

Group No. 2416 New Tinted Jardinieres

GROUP No. 2416 Contains:
- ⅔ doz. (8 only) No. 206—8½ inch Bon-Ton Jard.
- ⅔ " (8 only) " 233—8½ " Sylvan "
- ⅔ " (8 only) " 214—8½ " Bon-Ton "

PRICE FOR 2 Doz. 26.00 List

ONE-HALF GROUP NO. 2416 (1 doz.) $13.00 LIST

No. 206—Bon-Ton 9½ in. across top Doz., $18.00 · No. 233—Sylvan 9½ in. across top Doz., $24.00 · No. 214—Bon-Ton 9½ in. across top Doz., $18.00

Group No. 2516 New Tinted Jardinieres

GROUP No. 2516 Contains:
- ½ doz. (6 only) No. 206—9½ inch Bon-Ton Jard.
- ½ " (6 only) " 233—9½ " Sylvan "
- ½ " (6 only) " 214—9½ " Bon-Ton "

PRICE FOR 1½ doz. 30.00 List

ONE-HALF GROUP NO. 2516 (9 only) $15.00 LIST

No. 233—Sylvan 10½ in. across top, doz., $36.00; 11½ " 54.00 · No. 206—Bon-Ton 10½ in. across top, doz., $27.00; 11½ " 45.00 · No. 214—Bon-Ton 10½ in. across top, doz., $27.00; 12 " 54.00

Group No. 2616
Elegantly Tinted-Ivory Finished Jardinieres

GROUP No. 2616 Contains:
- 4 only No. 233—10½ in. Sylvan Jard.
- 4 " " 206—10½ " Bon-Ton "
- 4 " " 214—10½ " Bon-Ton "

PRICE 1 doz. ONLY $30.00 List

ONE-HALF GROUP NO. 2616 (6 only) $15.00 LIST

No. 2330—Sylvan Jardiniere and Pedestal Jar. 6½ in., Ped. 6½ in., each $1.00; Jar. 11½ in., Ped. 17 in., each $10.50

No. 2620—Bon-Ton Jardiniere and Pedestal Jar., 10½ in.; Ped. 15 in., each $6.00

No. 2140—Bon-Ton Jardiniere and Pedestal Jar. 12 in., Ped. 17 in., each $9.00

Group No. 2716 contains
- 1 only No. 2330 6½x 6½ J. & P.
- 1 only No. 2330 11½x17 J. & P.
- 1 only No. 2620 10½x15 J. & P.
- 1 only No. 2140 12 x17 J. & P.

4 Pieces $26.00 List

PRICE INCLUDES BOTH JARDINIERE & PEDESTAL COMPLETE.

Special

One Gross Equally Assorted	6½, 7½, 8½ and	9½ in.	Sylvan	Jardinieres,	$162.00	list.
" " " "	7½, 8½, 9½ "	10½	"	"	"	252.00	"
" " " "	6½, 7½, 8½ "	9½	"	Bon-Ton	"	120.00	"
" " " "	7½, 8½, 9½ "	10½	"	"	"	192.00	"

TRIAL GROUP NO. 1916

For the convenience of buyers wishing to see the entire line before ordering quantities we offer

1 each of all items shown on this page

25 Pieces (Jar & Ped counts as one piece) $60.00 List

The Brush-McCoy Pottery Co., Zanesville, Ohio., U. S. A.

Mitusa
TRADE MARK

CATALOGUE No. 16   SHEET 16G

"VOGUE" THE FASHION in Pottery.---The most striking and artistic line produced this year.---No store complete without every piece of this ware.

No. V116—Jardiniere—Vogue
12 inch....Dozen $72.00
14 inch....Dozen 126.00
Fine for Porch or Lawn

No. V222—Jardiniere—"Vogue"
5¼ inch....Dozen $7.50
6¼ inch....Dozen 9.00
7¼ inch....Dozen 13.50
8½ inch....Dozen 19.50
9 inch....Dozen 27.00
10 inch....Dozen 36.00
11 inch....Dozen 54.00
11¼ inch....Dozen 72.00

No. V213—Jardiniere—Vogue
8½ in., dz., $27.00 12¼ in., dz., $90.00
9½ in., dz., 36.00 14 in., dz., 144.00
10½ in., dz., 54.00

No. V89—Fern Dish—Vogue
7 in., with liner doz., $18.00

No. V97—Spill
Vogue
9 in high, $18.00
11 in high, 36.00
12 in high, 54.00

No. V046—Spill
Vogue
9 in high, doz., $18.00
12 in high, doz., 36.00
15 in high, doz., 54.00

No. V92—Fern Dish—Vogue
8 in. with liner, doz., $27.00

No. V453—Hanging Basket
Vogue
7 in., with chain, doz., $54.00

No. V1166—Jard. & Ped.—Vogue
Jard., 12 in; Ped, 20 in., ea. $18.00
Jard., 14 in; Ped, 23 in., ea. 27.00

No. V2229—Jardinere and Pedestal
Vogue
Jard. 11¾ in across top; Ped.
15¾ in. high. Each $13.50

No. V74—Umbrella Jard.—Vogue
23 in. high; each $9.00

No. V2130—Jard. and Ped—Vogue
Jard., 16 in; Ped. 26 in.; ea. $30.00

46

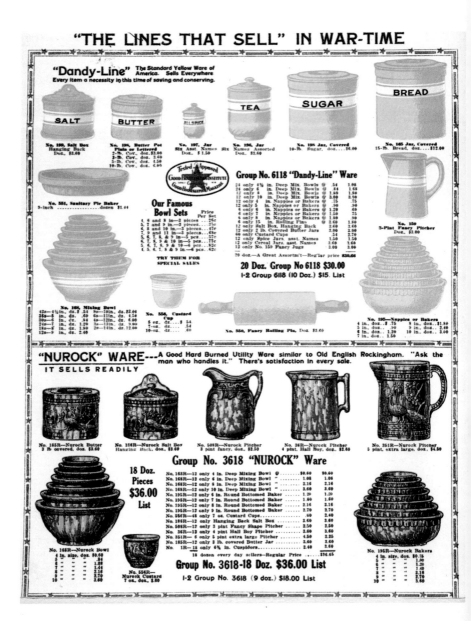

"Dandy-Line"
The Standard Yellow Ware of America. Sells Everywhere
Every item a necessity in this time of saving and conserving.

No. 199, Salt Box
Hanging Back
Doz., $2.60

No. 196, Butter Pot
Plain or Lettered
2-lb. Cov., doz..$2.00
3-lb. Cov., doz.. 2.40
5-lb. Cov., doz.. 2.50
10-lb. Cov., doz.. 4.00

No. 197, Jar
Six Asst. Names
Doz., $1.50

No. 196, Jar
Six Names Assorted
Doz., $2.50

No. 198 Jar, Covered
10-lb. Sugar, doz....$4.00

No. 165 Jar, Covered
15-lb. Bread, doz....$12.00

No. 551, Sanitary Pie Baker
9-inch ....dozen $1.44

Our Famous Bowl Sets
TRY THEM FOR SPECIAL SALES

Group No. 6118 "Dandy-Line" Ware

24 only 4½ in. Deep Mix. Bowls @	.54	1.08
24 only 6 in. Deep Mix. Bowls @	.84	1.68
12 only 8 in. Deep Mix. Bowls @	1.50	1.50
12 only 10 in. Deep Mix. Bowls @	3.00	2.50
12 only 6 in. Nappies or Bakers @	.75	.75
12 only 5 in. Nappies or Bakers @	.90	.90
6 only 6 in. Nappies or Bakers @	1.20	.60
6 only 7 in. Nappies or Bakers @	1.50	.75
6 only 8 in. Nappies or Bakers @	1.80	.90
6 only 15 in. Rolling Pins @	2.60	1.80
12 only Salt Box, Hanging Back	2.60	2.60
12 only 2 lb. Covered Butter Jars	2.00	2.00
60 only Custard Cups		.54	2.70
12 only Spice Jars, asst. Names		1.50	1.50
12 only Cereal Jars, asst. Names	2.60	2.60
12 only No. 159 Fancy Jugs	2.00	3.00

79 doz.—A Great Assort'm't—Reg'lar price $39.66

20 Doz. Group No 6118 $30.00
1-2 Group 6118 (10 Doz.) $15. List

No. 159
3-Pint Fancy Pitcher
Doz., $3.00

No. 165, Mixing Bowl
42z—4½ in., dz..$.54   9z—10in., dz..$3.04
24z—5 in., dz.. .60   6z—11in., dz.. 4.56
30z—6 in., dz.. .84   4z—12in., dz.. 6.00
24z—7 in., dz.. 1.20   3z—13in., dz.. 9.00
18z—8 in., dz.. 1.80   2z—14in., dz.. 12.00
12z—9 in., dz.. 2.40

No. 556, Custard Cup
5 oz., dz.....$.54
7-oz., dz..... .54
10-oz. dz..... .60

No. 556, Fancy Rolling Pin, Doz. $2.60

No. 195—Nappies or Bakers
4 in., doz..$.75   8 in., doz..$1.80
5 in., doz.. .90   9 in., doz.. 2.40
6 in., doz.. 1.20   10 in., doz.. 2.40
7 in., doz.. 1.50

"NUROCK" WARE---
A Good Hard Burned Utility Ware similar to Old English Rockingham. "Ask the man who handles it." There's satisfaction in every sale.
IT SELLS READILY

No. 185R—Nurock Butter
2 lb. covered, doz. $3.60

No. 156R—Nurock Salt Box
Hanging Back, doz. $3.60

No. 508R—Nurock Pitcher
3 pint fancy, doz., $2.50

No. 36R—Nurock Pitcher
4 pint Hall Boy, doz. $3.60

No. 351R—Nurock Pitcher
5 pint, extra large, doz. $4.50

Group No. 3618 "NUROCK" Ware

18 Doz. Pieces $36.00 List

No. 163R—12 only 4 in. Deep Mixing Bowl @	$0.60	$0.60
No. 163R—12 only 6 in. Deep Mixing Bowl "	1.08	1.08
No. 163R—12 only 8 in. Deep Mixing Bowl "	2.16	2.16
No. 163R—12 only 10 in. Deep Mixing Bowl "	3.60	3.60
No. 195R—12 only 6 in. Round Bottomed Baker	1.20	1.20
No. 195R—12 only 7 in. Round Bottomed Baker	1.50	1.50
No. 195R—12 only 8 in. Round Bottomed Baker	2.16	2.16
No. 195R—12 only 9 in. Round Bottomed Baker	2.70	2.70
No. 556R—48 only 7 oz. Custard Cups	.90	2.40
No. 156R—12 only Hanging Back Salt Box	2.60	3.60
No. 508R—12 only 3 pint Fancy Shape Pitcher	2.50	2.50
No. 36R—12 only 4 pint Hall Boy Pitcher	3.00	3.60
No. 351R— 6 only 5 pint extra large Pitcher	4.50	2.25
No. 185R—12 only 2 lb. covered Butter Jar	3.60	3.60
No. 1R—12 only 6¾ in. Cuspidors......	2.40	2.40

18 dozen every day sellers—Regular Price $36.65

Group No. 3618-18 Doz. $36.00 List
1-2 Group No. 3618 (9 doz.) $18.00 List

No. 165R—Nurock Bowl
4 in. size, dox. $0.60
5 " " .84
6 " " 1.44
7 " " 2.16
8 " " 2.70
10 " " 3.60

No. 556R—Nurock Custard
7 oz. doz. $.90

No. 195R—Nurock Bakers
4 in. size, doz. $0.75
5 " " 1.00
6 " " 1.20
7 " " 1.50
8 " " 2.16
9 " " 2.70
10 " " 3.60

The Brush-McCoy Pottery Co., Zanesville, Ohio, U. S. A.

Mitusa TRADE MARK

Our "White-Stone" Bristol Glazed Ware--Best Made.

No. 150 Willow Cereal Jars—Six names Assorted Gross $30.00   **No. 151 Willow Spice Jars—Any names or asst. Gross. $18.00**

No. 1501 Kitchen Sets---Each set consists of 6 Cereal Jars, 6 Spice Jars, (12 covered Pieces) per set   **$2.00**
Not less than 6 Sets to Package

No. 185—3 lb Butter Pot
Blue Tinted. Blue Letters
Gross. $30.00

		Not Balled	Balled
2 lb Blue Dec., gr.	$21.00	$22.50
3 lb " " "	27.00	28.50
5 lb " " "	36.00	32.40
10 lb " " "	54.00	50.00

No. 155—Butter Pot

No. 148—Tea Pot
Brown Glazed

48s dozen	$2.70
42s "	3.60
36s "	4.90
30s "	4.50
24s "	5.25

No. 162—Bean Pot
1 qt. Red & White dz., $2.10
2 " " " " " 2.70
3 " " " " " 3.36
4 " " " " " 4.50

No. 186—Stone Lid
Peacock—Salt Box
Blue Tinted. gr., $28.80

Salt

No. 162—Salt Box
Fancy Blue Dec.
Polished Wood Lid
Per gro., $43.20

No. 202s—Cuspidor
7 in. Brown or Blue
Gross $27.00

No. 205
Tall Peacock Cuspidor
Brown or Blue
Gross. $30.00

BEST BRISTOL CUSPIDORS
Group No. 5016

2 doz.	No. 202s Brown Dec.	7 in.
2 doz.	No. 5 Blue Dec.	7½ in.
2 doz.	No. 1 Blue Dec.	6½ in.
2 doz.	No. 14 Brown Dec.	7½ in.

8 DOZ. BIG VALUE CUSPIDORS
8 DOZ. IN GROUP $18.00 LIST

No. 1—Cuspidor
6½ in. Blue Dec., gr. $22.50

No. 014—Brown Cuspidor
7½ in. Ex. Val., gross. $28.80

No. 190
Pie Pan
Doz. $1.62

TRY THEM FOR SPECIAL SALES

No. 168s—Stirring Bowls
Actual Measure.

4 in. Blue Band, per dz.	$0.60
5 "	0.72
6 "	1.00
7 "	1.22
8 "	1.80
9 "	2.25
10 "	3.15
11 "	2.60
12 "	4.80

No. 195s—Nappies
Actual Measure.

4 in. Blue Tint, per dz.	$0.60
5 "	0.72
6 "	1.00
7 "	1.22
8 "	1.80
9 "	2.25
10 "	2.85

No. 193—Meat Roaster
11 in. Covered, dz., $4.32

No. 191—Baking Dish		
7 in. Open, Doz.,	$1.26
9 in. " "	1.62
11 in. " "	2.16

No. 192—Cooking Crock	
2 qt. Balled Open, Dz. $1.98
4 qt. " " " 2.52
6 qt. " " " 3.60

NO. 5116 SPECIAL COOKING SET

1—No. 191—	7 in.	Bake Pan
1—No. 190—	9 in.	Pie Pan
1—No. 191—	9 in.	Baking Dish
1—No. 192—	2 qt	Cooking Kettle
1—No. 193—11 in.		Roaster
1—No. 192—11 in.		Cover for Roaster
6 Pieces In Set		

PRICE ONLY
90 Cents
Per Set- -List
1 doz. sets to Package

Custard Cup
10 oz., dz., $0.72

Group No. 5316
FANCY PITCHERS
Here are the best lines of Staple Pitchers on the market. Group consists of

24 only No. 57—Blue Tint Jugs
24 only No. 29—Willow Tint Jugs
24 only No. 36—Hall Boy Jugs
24 only No. 53—Amsterdam Jugs

8 doz. Pitchers only $19.20 List

No. 36—Hall Boy Jug
4 Pt. Blue Dec.
Bristol Glaze; gr. $37.00

No. 57—Old Mill Jug
Blue Tint, 4 Pint
Per Gross, $30.00

No. 53—Amsterdam Jug
Blue Tinted & Decorated
4 Pint; gross $30.00

No. 29—Willow Tankard
4 Pt. Blue Tint Top
and Bottom, gr. $30.00

Best Line High Grade Cuspidors and Pitchers Made.

No. 366—Cuspidor
6 in. solid color
Gro. $25.20

No. 300—Cuspidor
7 in. Solid Colors
Brown and Green
Gro. $25.20

No. 10—Cuspidor
7½ in. Fine Blended Colors
Gro. $28.80

No. 59—Pitcher
2-3 pint; gro. $24.00

No. 132—Pitcher
1 pint; gro. $25.20

No. 38—Pitcher
1½ pint; gro. $22.50

No. 130—Pitcher
2 pint; gro. $28.80

GROUP NO.
2816
CONTAINS

{ 2½ doz. No. 366 Cuspidors, $2.10 $5.65
2½ " " 300 2.25 3.76
2½ " " 10 2.40 6.40

8 dozen fast selling cuspidors $18.00

PRICE
$18.00
LIST

1-2 GROUP NO. 2816—4 doz. Cuspidors—$9.75 List

GROUP NO.
3216
Contains

{ 2 doz. No. 59, Corn Pitchers,
2 " " 132, Green Woodland Pitchers, 1
2 " " 38, Green on Ivory Pitchers, 1½
2 " " 130, Brown Woodland Pitchers, 2

8 dozen Fancy Pitchers—A Fine Assort.

¾ Pint
1
1½
2

PRICE
$16.50
LIST

1-2 GROUP NO. 3216 (4 doz. Pitchers) Price $9.00 List

No. 319—Cuspidor
7½ in
Gro. $30.00

No. 302—Cuspidor
2 Color Glaze
7¼ in.; Gro. $51.30

No. 33—Copenhagen Jug
4 Pint Hand Decorated
Fine Colors Ivory Glaze.
Gro. $45.60

No. 43—Brown Glaze Jug
4 Pint; Gro. $30.00

No. 131—Pitcher
4 pint Green Woodland
Gro. $47.20

No. 52—Corn Pitcher
7½ in. High
Gro. $43.00

GROUP NO.
2916
CONTAINS

{ 2 doz. No. 101 Cuspidors, $2.70 $5.40
2.85 3.70
3.00 6.00

6 dozen Big Value Cuspidors. $17.10

PRICE
$17.10
LIST

1-2 GROUP NO. 2916—3 doz. Cuspidors—$9.30 List

GROUP
NO.
3316
Contains

{ 1½ doz. No. 43, Fancy Brown, Glazed 4 Pt. Jugs @ $2.50 $3.75
1½ " " 33, Copenhagen, 4 " " 3.75 5.62
1½ " " 131, Green Woodland, 4 " " 3.60 5.40
1½ " " 52, Corn Decorated 4 " " 3.75 5.62

6 dozen Fancy Jugs, all 4 Pint $20.40

PRICE
$20
LIST

1-2 GROUP NO. 3316 (3 doz. Jugs) Price List $10.80

No. 12—Cuspidor
7½ in. Woodland Green

No. 13—Cuspidor
Red Onyx
7¼ in.; Gro. $72.00

No. 3—Frog Cuspidor
8 in.; Gro. $45.00

No. 35—Tulip Jug
White Body
Finely Decorated
4 pint; Doz. $6.00

No. 55—Dutch Kid Jug
Green Glaze Outside
Cream Inside
4 Pint $4.80

Brown Woodland Jug
No. 131—4 Pint; Doz. $3.60

No. 1251—Grape Jug
4 Pint; Doz. $3.60
Tinted Top and Bottom; Grapes in
Natural Colors

GROUP NO.
3016
CONTAINS

{ 1½ doz. No. 3 Cuspidors, $3.75 $5.00
1½ " " 12 5.00 6.67
1½ " " 13 6.00 8.00

4 dozen Unique Cuspidors only $19.67

PRICE
19.50
LIST

1-2 GROUP NO. 3016—2 doz. Cuspidors—$10.00 List

Group No.
3416
Contains

{ 1 doz. No. 35, Tulip Pitcher, 4 Pint,
1 " " 55, Dutch Kid Jug, 4 Pint,
1 " " 131, Brown Woodland Jugs, 4 Pint,
1 " " 125, 1 Grape Decorated Jugs, 4 Pint,

1 dozen Fancy Pitchers or Jugs—Fig.

$6.00
4.50
3.00
3.60

PRICE
$18.00
LIST

1-2 GROUP NO. 3416 (2 doz. Jugs) Price $9.75

No. 13—Cuspidor
Cream White Body
Decoration Banded
7½ in. extra high.

No. 13—Cuspidor
Deco Cobalt Blue Glaze
Gold Decoration as shown
7¼ in. extra high. $6.75

No. 13—Cuspidor
Cream White Body
Deco. Wreath
7½ in.; Doz. $6.00

No. 34—Hall Boy
Blue Bird Deco
4 Pint; Doz. $6.00

No. 34—Hall Boy Jug
Blue and Gold
Gold Decoration
4 Pint; Doz. $6.75

No. 36—Hall Boy
Fleur-de-Lis Deco.
4 Pint; Doz. $6.00

GROUP NO.
3116
CONTAINS

{ 1 doz. No. 13, Blue and Gold
1 " " 13, White Dec.
1 " " 13, White Dec.

3 dozen Extra Fine Cuspidors

PRICE
$18.00
LIST

1-2 Above GROUP NO. 3116—(1½ doz.) List $9.75

GROUP NO.
3516
CONTAINS

{ ½ doz. No. 34, Blue Bird, 4 pint Pitchers
½ " " 34, Blue and Gold, 4 pint Pitchers
½ " " 36, Fleur de Lis, 4 pint Pitchers

PRICE
18.00
LIST

1-2 GROUP NO. 3516 (1½ doz. Pitchers) Price $9.75 List

OUR LUCILE TOILET---Fancy Shape---White Stone Body---Bristol Glaze.

No. 20—Lucile Ewer & Basin

9s Large size	White Stone, doz.	$12.00
9s Large size	Blue tint, doz.	13.60
9s Large size	Dec. & Gold, doz.	24.00
12s Small size	White stone, doz.	7.20
12s Small size	Blue tint.	7.50

No. 21—Lucile Chamber.

9s Large size	White stone, doz.	$3.60
9s Large size	Blue tint, doz.	3.90
9s Large size	Dec. & Gold, doz.	7.20
12s Small size	White stone, doz.	3.00
12s Small size	Blue tint, doz.	3.15

Above prices are open—if covered,
one-half for covers.

No. 17—Lucile Combinet

9s Large size	Covered Whitestone, doz.	$9.75
9s Large size	Covered Blue tint.	doz.	10.50
9s Large size	Covered Dec. & Gold., doz.	19.50

'PERFECTION' COMBINET

It's a Chamber.

Slop Jar

Combinet

No. 19—Chambers—Fluted

9s White open, gross.	$24.00
12s White, open.	22.20
9s Blue Tint open, gross	25.60
12s Blue Tint, open, gross	29.50

Covers one-half price of Chambers.

No. 500—"Perfection Combinet"
Full 9s size. Has wide Rolled Edge Top
for Chamber. Deep Finger Grip on
bottom for dumping. Nicely embossed. New Practical shape.
Plain White, doz. $19.60
Blue tint, doz. $21.60

Lucile Toilet Sets No. 2321

6 PIECE SET
Plain White, each · · · · $1.65
Blue Tint, each · · · · · 1.80
Blue Tint and decalcomania dec. · · · · 3.00
" · · · · · gold traced 3.20
6 Piece set consists of Ewer and Basin, Covered
Chamber, Mug and Slab.

10 PIECE SET
Plain White, each · · · $2.40
Blue Tint, each · · · · · 2.55
Blue Tint and decalcomania dec. · · · · 3.75
" · · · · · gold traced 4.20
10 Piece set consists of Ewer and Basin, Covered
Chamber, covered soap and drainer, mug,
mouth Ewer and Brush Vase.

12 PIECE SET
Plain White, each · · · $3.00
Blue Tint, each · · · · · 3.00
Blue Tint and decalcomania dec. · · · · 5.25
" · · · · · gold traced 5.70
12 Piece Set—Add combinet to 10 piece set.

CAT SOAP SLAB
Blue Tint

Gross $12.00

No. 17—Blue Tinted
9s size Covered doz. $10.50

No. 16—White Combinet
9s. Covered, $9.00 dozen.

2 DOZEN Full Size

12 only	No. 16	
3	"	16
3	"	16
3	"	16
3	"	16

White Cov'd. Rolled Combinets, full size
Blue Band Cov'd. Rolled Combinets, full size
Tint Band Cov'd. Rolled Combinets, full size
Green Stippled Cov'd. Rolled Combinets, full size
Lucile Blue Tint, Cov'd. Rolled Combinets, full size
Willow Blue Tint Cov'd. Rolled Combinets, full size

No. 18—Green Stippled
9s size, Covered, doz., $9.75

No. 16—Blue Tint
9s. size Covered, doz., $9.75

"BEATS ALL"
Combinet Group No. 5616
2 dozen only $18.00

No. 16—Blue Banded
9s. size Cov'd., doz., $9.75

ONLY
$18.00
List

No. 18—Blue Willow
9s size, per doz., $10.50

Any of the above combinets as well as any item in this Catalogue sold in open stock. Get Special Car Load Prices.

Birds, Bees, Butterflies, Bowls, Bird Baths, etc.

Handsomely Colored and Glazed Table Decorations.
Package of Wax with instructions with each shipment.

NOTE:—Birds are packed in cartons of six dozen, no charge. Other quantities upon six dozen. 5c per dozen extra for packing

No. 051 BIRD RED
Dz. $5.00

No. 051 BIRD BLUE
Dz. $5.00

No. 053 BIRD
Dz. $3.75

No. 053 BIRD
Dz. $3.75

No. 052 CANARY BIRD
Dz. $5.00

No. GW 057 TRAY
White with Black and Green Lines
11 in. Tray Only. Dz. $37.50
No. GV064 Block to match Dz. $7.50
Birds not included

No. GV066 BULB BOWL
White, Black and White
4 in. Bowl Only. Dz.
6 in. " " "
8 in. " " "
No. GV064 Block Dz. $7.50
Birds NOT included

No. 057 TRAY
White with Black and Green Lines
11 in. Tray Only. Dz. $37.50
No. GV064 Block to match Dz. $7.50
Birds not included

No. 059 BIRD
Assorted Color
Dz. $5.00

No. 060 FROG BLOCK
Mottled Green Glazed
Dz. $5.00

No. V058 BULB BOWL
Vogue, Black and White
4 in. Bowl Only. Dz. $7.50
6 in. " " " $7.50
8 in. " " "
12 in. " " "
No. V064 Block to match

No. 0100 PEDESTAL AND TRAY
Crazy Mint Glaze
Price complete (2 Pieces), no Birds
Each $5.00

No. 057 TRAY OR BIRD BATHS
Assorted Colors
8 in. Tray Only. Dz. $7.50
11 in. Tray Only. Dz. $22.50
No. 064 Block to match Dz. $3.00
Birds NOT included

NOTE:—Birds, Bees and Butterflies are attached with wax...not included in price of Trays. Illustrations show manner of attaching for attractive display.

No. 058 BULB BOWL
Assorted Colors
4 in. Bowl Only. Dz.
6 in. " " "
8 in. " " "
12 in. " " "
No. 064 Block Dz. $3.00

No. 061 TURTLE BLOCK
Mottled Mat Green
Glaze Dz. $5.00

No. 058 BULB BOWL
Assorted Colors
4 in. Bowl Only. Dz. $3.75
6 in. " " " $7.50
8 in. " " " $10.00
12 in. " " " $15.00
No. 064 Block Dz. $3.00

No. 063 BEE
Vanity Box
Assorted Colors
Dz. $5.00

No. 062 BUTTERFLY
Vanity Box
Assorted Colors
Dz. $5.00

No. 064 BIRD
Vanity Box
Assorted Colors
Dz. $5.00

No. 0850 COMBINATION
Ring Holder Tray
Assorted Colors
Dz. $12.50

No. 081 POPPY TRAY
Assorted Colors
6½ in. Tray Only. Dz.
4 in. " " "
6 in. " " "
12 in. " " "
No. 064 Block to match Dz. $3.00
Bees and Butterflies NOT included

No. 058 BULB BOWL
Assorted Colors
4 in. Bowl Only. Dz. $3.75
6 in. " " " $7.50
8 in. " " " $10.00
12 in. " " " $15.00
No. 064 Block Dz. $3.00

No. 085 RING HOLDER
Assorted Colors
Complete Dz. $8.75

No. 052 BLACK BIRD
Dz. $5.00

No. 055 BUTTERFLY
Dz. $3.00

No. 053 WHITE BIRD
Dz. $5.00

No. 064 BUTTERFLY
Brown or Yellow
Dz. $3.00

No. 049 BEE
Decorated
Dz. $3.00

No. 057 TRAYS OR BIRD BATHS
Assorted Colors
8 in. Tray Only. Dz. $7.50
11 in. Tray Only. Dz. $22.50
No. 064 Block Dz. $3.00
Birds NOT included

No. 056 SUNFLOWER TRAY
Assorted Colors
8 in. Tray Only. Dz. $7.50
No. 064 Block to fit
Bees and Butterflies NOT included

No. 058 BULB BOWL
Assorted Colors
4 in. Bowl Only. Dz. $3.75
6 in. " " " $7.50
8 in. " " " $10.00
12 in. " " " $15.00
No. 064 Block Dz. $3.00

No. 055 BUTTERFLY
Dz. $3.00

No. 050 BIRD ON BRANCH
Assorted Colors
Dz. $6.00

"BRUCO" WARE---
GOOD HARD BODY AND GLAZE---NOT SEMI-PORCELAIN BUT JUST AS GOOD FOR ALL PRACTICAL PURPOSES---CREAM WHITE COLOR WELL FINISHED.

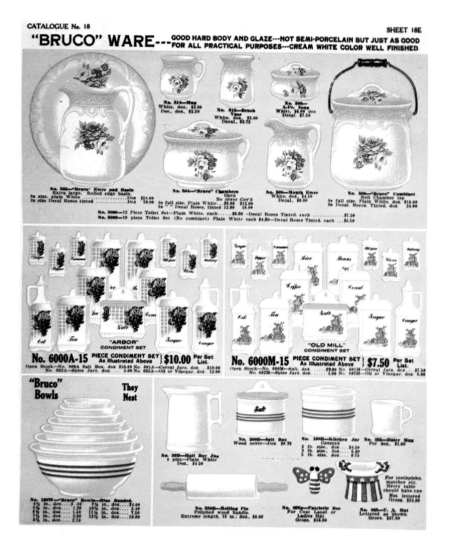

No. 454—"Vista"
Hanging Basket
7 in., with chains
Doz., $60.00

No. 042—"Vista" Vase
Hand decorated
11 in. high; doz. $36.00

No. 02—"Vista" Vase
12 in. high; doz. $54.00

No. 455—"Vista" Wall
Pocket
Hand decorated
12 in. high; doz. $63.00

No. L455—Hanging Basket.
"Lotus Ware."
7", Green or Gray
around panels, dz. $60.00
With chains.

No. L042—Vase.
"Lotus."
Green or Gray
around Panels
11" high, dz. $30.00

No. V92—Fern Dish Vogue
8 in. Black lines, doz. $27.00

No. V040—Spill
"Vogue"
Black panels
9" high, dz. $18.00
12" " " $36.00
15" " " $54.00

No. 62—"Vista" Umbrella
Stand
21 in. high; 9 in. opening
Hand decorated
Each, $9.00

No. 2400—"Vista" Jardiniere and
Pedestal.
Jar., 10 in. opening; 11½ in. bulge.
Ped., 17 in. high; each $12.00
No. 240—"Vista" Jardiniere
7 in. opening, 8⅛ in. bulge, doz. $18.00
8 " 9⅝ " " 27.00
9 " 10⅝ " " 42.00
10 " 11½ " " 60.00

No. L2350—Jardiniere and Pedestal.
"Lotus"
Jard.—10 in. opening, 11½ in. bulge.
Ped.—17 in. high.—each $10.00
No. L235—Jardiniere—Lotus.
Green or Gray around Ivory Panels
6 in. opening, 7⅛ in. bulge, doz. $10.00
7 " 8⅛ " " 15.00
8 " 9⅝ " " 22.50
9 " 10⅝ " " 33.00
10 " 11½ " " 50.00

No. M2390—Jardiniere and Pedestal
"Monochrome."
Beautiful Neutral Gray—White Birds
Jard.—10 in. opening, 11½ in. bulge.
Ped.—17 in. high—each $10.00
No. M239—Jardiniere.
5 in. opening, 6 in. bulge, doz. $ 7.50
6 " 7⅛ " " 10.00
7 " 8⅛ " " 15.00
8 " 9⅝ " " 22.50
9 " 10⅝ " " 33.00
10 " 11½ " " 50.00

No. V2130—Jardiniere and Pedestal
"Vogue."
Jard., 14 in.; Ped. 26 in.; each $20.00
No. V213—Jardiniere—"Vogue"
8½ in. dia., $27.00 12½ in. dia., $90.00
9½ " dia., 36.00 14 " dia., 144.00
10½ " dia. 54.00

53

BEAUTIFULLY COLORED GLAZED JARDINIERES---BEST MADE

No. 1018 "Metropolitan" Group

One Gross---1 Doz. each 7½, 8½, 9½, 10½ in. Nos. 117, 237, and 202 equally assorted.

12 Doz Blended Jard's — GROUP No. 1018 — $90.00 List

Per doz. asst. as in Group 1018, $8.00 List

No. 237—Jardiniere

7 in.	Blended, Doz.	$4.50
8 in.	" "	7.00
9 in.	" "	10.50
10 in.	" "	15.00
11½ in.	" "	27.00

No. 117—Jardiniere

7½ in.	Doz.	$4.50
8½ in.	"	7.00
9½ in.	"	10.50
10½ in.	"	15.00
11½ in.	"	27.00

No. 202—Jardiniere

6¼ in.	Doz.	$2.16
7½ in.	"	5.00
8½ in.	"	8.00
9½ in.	"	12.00
10½ in.	"	18.00
11½ in.	"	40.00

"Liberty" Group No. 1218

No. 214—Jardiniere

6½ in.	Doz.	$2.40
7½ in.	"	6.00
8½ in.	"	9.00
9¾ in.	"	15.00
10½ in.	"	24.00
12½ in.	"	45.00

No. 1118 "Pittsburgh" Group

One Gross-3 Doz. each No. 239-6½ in. (Green, Blue, Brown) No. 117--7½, 8½, 9½, No. 237--7½, 8½, 9½ and No. 202--7½, 8½, 9½ Jardinieres

12 Doz Blended Jard's — GROUP No. 1118 — $67.50 List

Per doz. asst. as in Group 1118. $5.75 List

No. 228—Jardiniere

7½ in.	Doz.	$6.00
8½ in.	"	9.00
9½ in.	"	15.00
10¾ in.	"	27.00

HIGH-GRADE BLENDED JARDINIERES

No	239—2	only Blended Jardinieres	6½	in across top
"	214—2	" "	6½	" " "
"	202—2	" "	6½	" " "
"	228—2	" "	7¾	" " "
"	237—2	" "	7½	" " "
"	117—2	" "	7¾	" " "
"	239—2	" "	8⅝	" " "
"	228—2	" "	8¾	" " "
"	214—2	" "	9⅝	" " "
"	202—2	" "	9¾	" " "
"	117—2	" "	10¾	" " "
"	237—2	" "	10⅝	" " "

24 Blended Jardinieres

Best Values Best Selling Sizes, Highly Colored and Glazed.

"Liberty" Group No. 1218
2 dozen
$15.00 List
1-2 Group 1218
1 doz. $8. List

No. B239—Jardiniere

3"	opening.	4¼"	bulge, doz.	$1.00
4"	"	5¼"	" "	1.50
5"	"	6¼"	" "	2.00
6"	"	7¼"	" "	3.00
7"	"	8¼"	" "	6.00
8"	"	9½"	" "	10.00
9"	"	10½"	" "	15.00
10"	"	11½"	" "	25.00

No. 2370—Jar and Pedestal
Jard. 11½" across top
Pedestal 16 in. high
Price complete $4.05

No. 2780—Jardiniere and Pedestal
11" Jard.; 18" Ped.
Complete, $5.25

No. 1170—Jar and Pedestal
Jard. 7½" across top
Pedestal 7½" high
Price complete 75c
—Also—
11½" Jar: 18" Ped
$4.80

No. 2020—Jar and Pedestal
Jard. 8½" across top
Ped. 9" high; $1.50
—Also—
11½" Jar: 18" Ped.
$4.50

"Matchless" Group No. 1318 Blended Jardinieres and Pedestals

Contents

1—	7½"	Jar with	7½" Ped
1	8½"	" "	9 " "
1—	9½"	" "	12½" "
1	10¼"	" "	15 " "
1	11½"	" "	16 " "
1	12 "	" "	18 " "

6 Complete Jars & Peds $18.00 List

No. B2390—Jardiniere and Pedestal. "Blended"
Jard. 10" opening.
11½" bulge.
Ped., 17" high
Complete, each $5.00

No. 2140—Jar and Pedestal
Jard. 12" across top
Pedestal, 17" high
Price complete $6.00

"Princess" Group, No. 1418-10c, 15c, 20c and 25c Glazed Jars

No. 2370—Jardiniere

3"	opening.	4¼"	bulge, dz.	$1.00
4"	"	5¼"	" "	1.50
5"	"	6¼"	" "	2.00

No. 202—Jardiniere
6¼" across top
Per doz., $2.10

12	No. 239	Col. Glazed Jars	3⅝"	across	bulge
12	" 233	" " "	3½"	"	top
12	" 239	" " "	4⅝"	"	bulge
12	" 233	" " "	4½"	"	top
6	" 239	" " "	5⅝	"	bulge
6	" 233	" " "	5½"	"	top
6	" 202	" " "	6¼"	"	"
6	" 217	" " "	6½"	"	"

6 Doz. Princess Jars $9.00 List

No 217—Jardiniere
6½" across top
Per doz $2.25

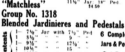

No. 233G—Jardiniere

		Doz
3½"	Green Glaze	$1.00
4½"	" "	1.50
5½"	" "	2.00
6½"	" "	3.00

THESE DEVICES HAVE BEEN PRONOUNCED BY PHYSICIANS AND FOOD EXPERTS EVERYWHERE AS ABSOLUTELY THE BEST METHOD FOR MAKING PURE, HEALTHFUL, INVIGORATING, DELICIOUS COFFEE. POTS, DRIPPER AND PLATES ARE OF CHINA OR EARTHENWARE, AND VASTLY SUPERIOR TO METAL POTS. NO UNSANITARY SACKS, OR ANYTHING LIABLE TO CONTAMINATE COFFEE IS USED. NOTE THAT YOU CAN SECURE IN THIS LINE DEVICES FROM THE BEAUTIFUL SILVER DECORATED POT, TO THE GARDINER SINGLE-DRIP, CHEAPEST DRIP DEVICE ON THE MARKET.

THE GARDINER PATENT — COFFEE MAKERS
Double-Drip and Single-Drip

SHEET N 25

No. 364H GARDINER 5-CUP
PATENT DOUBLE-DRIP
CHINA COFFEE POTS

These pots are made from vitrified China- White-Blue-Brown-Green - may be had either Plain or Beautifully Silver Decorated.

No. 364H - Plain - Not Decorated
White not decorated doz. $40.00
Green or Brown plain doz. $50.00
Blue not decorated doz. $54.00

No. 364H-SILVER DECORATED
White - Decorated doz. $54.00
Green or Brown dec'd doz. $60.00
Blue decorated doz. $64.80

Complete with Disks, Post, instructions for use.

No. 366W GARDINER 7-CUP
PATENT DOUBLE-DRIP
"WHITESTONE" COFFEE POTS

These Pots are designed for folks who wish a larger and cheaper pot than the China. They will make perfect coffee. Are made of hard burned glazed earthen ware, nice shape and will give satisfaction.

No. 366W-7 Cup pot, Natural White dz. $30.00
No. 366W-7 cup Brown white lined dz. $36.00
No. 366W-7 cup Blue white lined dz. $42.00

Complete with Disks and instructions.

PARTS FOR ALL GARDINER POTS

Extra Porcelain Disks-fit all
Gardiner Pots - per doz. $2.00
POSTS - Complete-fit all pots doz. $4.50
Note-No. 364H and 366W take Nos. 1, 2 & 3 disks.
No. 370W takes Nos. 1 and 2 only—No. 1 for Coffee and No. 2 for Tea.

DELICIOUS
COFFEE & TEA

Easily, Cheaply, Quickly
Made by the

GARDINER
SINGLE-DRIP
COFFEE AND
TEA MAKER

CHEAPEST PRACTICAL DRIP
COFFEE MAKER EVER OFFERED

Designed and manufactured for lovers of Drip Coffee and Tea who can not afford an expensive make. Use with your old Coffee Pot or any vessel in which it will fit, a china or earthenware pitcher is very good. Our No. 368 Hall Boy Jug is excellent.

No. 370W-Coffee & Tea Maker
Natural White doz. $12.00
Blue Tint doz. $13.20
Dec'd. like above doz. $14.40

No. 2736W - Complete
Consist of No. 370W Decorated and No. 368 Jug to match with disk, etc. doz. $18.00

Complete with full directions for use.

THREE TOP-NOTCH SPECIALS FOR EVERY STORE--LOOK 'EM OVER--THEY'RE GOOD.

EGYPTIAN JARDINIERES

No. 243E - JARDINIERES
"EGYPTIAN"

Beautiful Semi-Mat Finish
Colors—Green, Blue and Salmon

4½ in. doz. $3.00   9 in. doz. $13.50
6 in. doz. 4.50   10 in. doz. 21.00
7 in. doz. 6.00   11 in. doz. 30.00
8 in. doz. 9.00   either color in any size.

GROUP NO. { 6 only 4 in. } 2 Dozen
6425E   {   }   for
2 DOZEN {   10   } $21.00
         {   11   }

BULB BOWL SPECIAL

No. 095PV BOWL

Unique shape finished in semi-mat glazed colors.

Blue-Green-Fawn

Makes a fine bowl at an exceptionally low price. Try one of these assortments.

No. 095PV Bulb Bowl
2 inch doz. $1.44
4 "   "   1.80
5 "   "   2.50
6 "   "   3.60
7 "   "   6.00

No. 095PV Bulb Bowls in Nests
No. 0095PV-Nest consists of one each 3, 4, 5, 6, & 7 in. Bowls - Per Doz. Nests only $35.00

GROUP No. 5625PV-With Blocks

1 doz. each 3-4-5-6 & 7 in. Bowls
1 doz. Blocks to match 6 & 7 in. Bowls
6 DOZ. PIECES   ONLY $16.67

HIGH-GLAZED HARD BURNED
FANCY SPECIALS

No. 302H-Cuspidor-7 in. **No. 1X-Cuspidor-7 in.**
Green, Brown or Blue   Green, Brown or Blue
dozen $3.75   dozen $7.20

GROUP No. 6325 - SPECIAL

1 doz. No. 302H Cuspidors   **ONLY**
½ doz. No. 1X Cuspidors
1 doz. No. 508X Pitchers   **$18.00**
½ doz. No. 331X Pitchers
3 DOZ. High Glazed Specials   **LIST**

No. 508X-Pitcher-3 Pint   **No. 331X Pitcher 4 Pint**
Colors Green, Blue or   Colors Green, Brown or
Brown Onyx doz. $7.20   Blue Doz. $8.40

FLORASTONE

A new treatment on our popular "Stonecraft" line. Shapes are Artistic Colonial - Body high fired gray stone - Decorations in Rich High Gloss Colors - A truly beautiful creation.

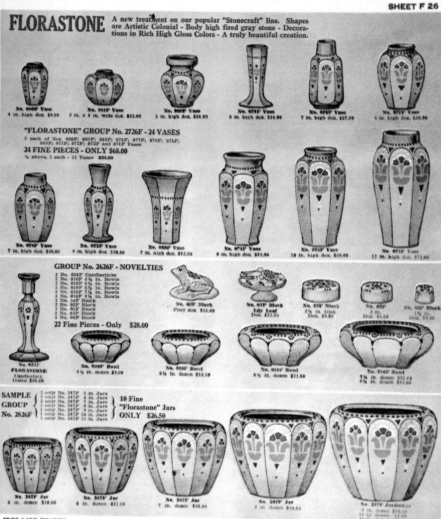

"FLORASTONE" GROUP No. 2726F - 24 VASES

2 each of Nos. 060F; 061F; 063F; 076F; 077F; 078F; 075F; 069F; 071F; 072F; 073F and 074F Vases

24 FINE PIECES - ONLY $68.00

½ above, 1 each - 12 Vases $34.00

GROUP No. 2626F - NOVELTIES

2 No. 034F Candlesticks
2 No. 010F 4¾ in. Bowls
2 No. 010F 5¼ in. Bowls
2 No. 010F 6¼ in. Bowls
2 No. 010F 7¼ in. Bowls
2 No. 010F 7¾ in. Bowls
2 No. 56F Block
2 No. 02F Block
2 No. 05F Block
2 No. 03F Block
2 No. 04F Block

22 Fine Pieces - Only $28.00

SAMPLE GROUP No. 2826F
2 only No. 247F 5 in. Jars
2 only No. 247F 6 in. Jars
2 only No. 247F 7 in. Jars
1 only No. 247F 8 in. Jars
1 only No. 247F 9 in. Jars
1 only No. 247F 10 in. Jars
1 only No. 247F 11 in. Jars

10 Fine "Florastone" Jars ONLY $26.50

1926 LIST PRICES

"WISE BIRDS" -- A New Line of "Purse-Openers" for Every Store Everywhere.
Finely Modeled - Richly Colored - Attractive - Novel - Reasonably priced.

No. 0140L - Decorative Owl
Furnished in 4 sizes:
Either Finish
7 in. high doz. $ 9.00
8 in. high doz. 12.00
9 in. high doz. 18.00
10 in. high doz. 27.00
Also made in Pastel No. 0140P

No. 0136P - Bottle with Cork
Furnished in two finishes:
No. 0136P Pastel doz. $30.00
No. 0136L Majolica doz. $30.00
Patented Nov. 30, 1926

No. 0139P - Pitcher
Pours from beak.
Furnished in two finishes:
No. 0139P Pastel doz. $36.00
No. 0139L Majolica doz. $36.00

No. 0143P - Wall Vase - 8 in.
For Cut Flowers
Furnished in two finishes:
No. 0143P Pastel doz. $12.00
No. 0143L Majolica doz. $12.00

No. 0141L-Flower Vase-8½ in.
Furnished in two finishes:
No. 0141L Majolica doz. $30.00
No. 0141P Pastel doz. $30.00

NOTE—The letter "P" after number denotes that article
is finished in soft Pastel Semi-Mat. Finish.
"L" denotes Majolica High Gloss Finish.

No. 0135P - 8 oz. Owl Beakers per doz. $3.00

No. 6002P - Owl Bottle Set
Consists of 1 No. 0136P Owl Bottle with Cork
and 4 No. 0135P Owl 8 oz. Beakers
Price per dozen sets $42.00

No. 0142L - Owl Book Ends
Beautiful High Gloss Majolica finish
7 in. high per dozen pairs $45.00
Also Made in Pastel (No. 0142P)
Per dozen pairs $54.00

No. 7002P - Owl Pitcher Sets
Consists of 1 No. 0139P Owl Handled Pitcher
and 4 No. 0135P Owl 8 oz. Beakers
Price per dozen sets $42.00

DON'T MISS ANY ITEM HERE - ALL GOOD ONES

No. 055X Fern - Onyx
5 in. with liner doz. $12.00

No. 055Z - Fern - Indian
5 in. with liner doz. $18.00

No. 0199X - "Bug" Door Stop
A Genuine Novelty, Finely Modeled and
Beautifully Colored 9 in. long doz. $24.00

No. 71X Umbrella Stand
20½ in. high-9½ in. wide
Furnished in Red, Blue,
or Green Onyx
Doz. either color $54.00

No. 094X Vase
For Cut Flowers or
one bulb
7 in. high doz. $15.00

No. 0676M - Special
3¼ in. Bowl
1¾ in. Block
in set
Per doz. Sets $3.33

No. 0676X - Special
3¼ in. Bowl
1¾ in. Block
in set
Per doz. sets $3.75

No. 071 - Bird-on-Perch
Flower Block
Assorted Colors
3¼ in. high doz. $7.50

No. 71M Umbrella Stand
Furnished in Green only
20½ in. high doz. $45.00

1927 LIST PRICES

"FLORODORA" BULB LOGS
For Bulbs or
Cut Flowers
No. 0124D-6 in.
Bulb Log
Beautifully
Finished
Dozen $12.00

High Gloss or Mat as Preferred

No. 0125D - 9½ in. BULB LOG
"FLORODORA" Finish Doz. $18.00

Holds
Matches
Pencil
Ashes
Cards

And
Marks
The
Tables

4½ in. High, 4 in. Wide
**No. 0121 Combination
Card Table Marker**
Numbered from 1 to 6
Per Set of 6 Pcs. List $6.00
Per Doz. Any Nos. $13.50

HERE'S SOME GOOD ITEMS
FOR THE GIFT COUNTER.
**No. 0120G "STAR"
Card Table Markers**
Art Pottery Glazed — 6 in Set — Numbered from
1 to 6 — Holds Lead Pencil — Ashes — Marks
Tables — Set of 6 — $1.33.
Open Stock — Any Numbers — Per Dozen $3.00

No. 010T "CACTI" Bowl
Unique New Finish
Colors-Blue, Brown, Green
High Gloss Glazes
4½ in. per dozen $ 3.00
5½ in. per dozen   6.00
6½ in. per dozen 10.50
7½ in. per dozen 15.00
8½ in. per dozen 22.50
Blocks: 02T $1.80; 05T $3.60

Unique Owl Book Ends
No. 0142P - Pastel Glaze per doz. pairs $54.00
No. 0142L - Majolica Glaze per doz. pairs $48.00
7 in. high - Artistically Modeled

Novelty Elephant Book Ends
Natural Colors — Ivory Tusks
No. 0126P - Natural Colors
Doz. pairs $36.00

Mat Green Elephant Book Ends
Fine Mat Green Glazed
No. 0126M - 5 in. doz. pairs $27.00

No. 0127V Venetian Book Ends
Rich Brown on Artistic Stone Body
Per dozen pairs $24.00

GROUP No. 1328   1 Pair each Nos. 0142P - 0142L
0125P - 0126M and 0127V — 5
pairs fine Book ends in Group.   **Price List $15.00**

FINE FOR GIFTS-FAVORS-PREMIUMS AND REGULAR SALE

BEST AMERICAN WORKS--
30 Hour movements in dust-proof
cases-wound set and regulated from
back-Gives perfect satisfaction.

Patented Oct. 21, 1924
No. 333X "JUG-TIME" Clock
The Famous Art Pottery Onyx Finish
A Distinct Novelty-Finished in Red, Blue
or Green Onyx.   Weighs 4 pounds.
Price-Packed singly-either
color or assorted Per Doz. **$36.00**
No. 333X is 6¾ in. high-5¼ in. wide.

No. 336X "FLAPPER" Clock
This little beauty is a big winner every-
where---made in Red Onyx, Blue and
Green Onyx.
Weight only 3 pounds.
Price-Packed singly either
color or assorted Per Doz. **$30.00**
No. 336X is 4½ in. high-4 in. wide

No. 337L-OWL CLOCK-Fancy dial and hands
Here's the very latest in fancy clocks. It is wonderfully
modeled and finished.
Packed in mailable carton weighing only 5 pounds.
No. 337L—High Gloss Glazed Majolica Color as above
No. 337P—Soft Pastel semi-gloss Glaze, see set as below
No. 337 is 7¼ in. high and 6½ in. wide   **$48.00**

No. 3329X 3-Piece Console Sets
Each Set consists of one "Jug-Time"
Clock and 2 Candlesticks
Price-Packed 1 set in mail-
able carton-Per Doz. Sets **$48.00**

No. 3336X Mantel or Bureau Set
Each Set consists of "Flapper Clock"
and 2 Candlesticks.
Price-Packed 1 set in mailable carton Per Doz. Sets **$39.00**

No. 3325P - BOUDOIR CLOCK SET
Each Set consists of Clock and 2 Candle Holders
Packed one set in carton-made in two finishes.
Weight 6 Pounds   Per Doz. Sets
No. 3325L—High Gloss Majolica Ware
No. 3325P—Pastel Finish as illustrated **$60.00**

The Brush Pottery Co., Zanesville Ohio, U. S. A.

NEW ITEMS! DON'T MISS ANY OF THESE
EVERY ONE A SELLER-PROFIT MAKER

SHEET H28

ART GLAZED DUTCH JUG AND MUGS.

No. 611-W Fancy Grape Jug

NEW BANDS - EXTRA FINE WARE

FOR PREMIUMS AND SPECIAL SALES!

No. 143Y Blue Banded

"KOLORKRAFT" BRINGS CHEER TO THE KITCHEN

TAKE ADVANTAGE OF PRESENT COLOR FAD — OUR NEW WARE THAT — BE THE FIRST TO SHOW IT

1928 LIST PRICES

60

UNIQUE NOVELTIES FROM OUR RESEARCH LABORATORIES

"MYSTIC" RADIO SETS—Mounted in Art Pottery

They are of the Crystal type—require nothing but head phones, aerial and ground. They are made to use for local reception only, and we do not sell or recommend them for use more than ten to twenty miles from Broadcasting Stations depending on power of Stations. They will get local Stations LOUD and CLEAR—Singularly free from Static.

GENUINE NOVELTIES—Every Fan Wants One—Make Fine Favors and Presents— Each one packed in mailable carton.

No. 702—"Bug" Finished in Brown, Blue or Green Onyx Glaze Price each $6.00
No. 701—Rolling Pin—Finished in "Dandy-Line Yellow" Price each $4.00
No. 700—Wall Pocket Finished in Blue, Green or Brown Glaze Price each $6.00
SAMPLE GROUP No. 3027-3 Only No. 702-3 Only No. 700; 1 Only No. 701-6 For $35.00

No. 702X "BUG" RADIO SET
Patent Allowed.

No. 701 - ROLLING PIN MYSTIC RADIO SET.
This Set is mounted entirely within our regular Yellow Rolling Pin.

PLEASE NOTE The above sets are of approved Crystal Type—do not require any batteries or tubes. We do not furnish head phones—these can be obtained at small cost from any radio dealer. Complete instructions are packed with each set. They will last a life time.

No. 700X WALL POCKET
Patented Sept. 14, 1926.

UNIQUE BEAUTIFUL ART CLOCKS

FINE FOR GIFTS-FAVORS-PREMIUMS AND REGULAR SALE
BEST AMERICAN WORKS—RELIABLE

NEW!

MANY THOUSANDS SOLD!

30 Hour movements in dust-proof cases-wound set and regulated from back-Gives perfect satisfaction.

Patented Oct. 21, 1924.
No. 333X "JUG-TIME" Clock
The Famous Art Pottery Onyx Finish A Distinct Novelty-Finished in Red, Blue or Green Onyx. Packed in individual mailing cartons. Weighs 4 pounds.
Price-Packed singly either color or assorted Per Doz. **$36.00**
No. 333X is 6¾ in. high-5¼ in. wide.

No. 336X "FLAPPER" Clock
This little beauty is a big winner everywhere—made in Red Onyx, Blue and Green Onyx. Packed in individual mailing carton. Weight only 3 pounds.
Price-Packed singly either color or assorted Per Doz. **$30.00**
No. 336X is 4½ in. high-4 in. wide

HERE'S THE QUEEN OF THEM ALL!   NOTE THE NEW "HEARTBEAT"

No. 338K "SWEETHEART" ART CLOCK
Beautiful Hichroa Rose Color Glaze — Fancy "Heartbeat" Movement—Brass Finish Chain 5 x 5 in.
Packed one in Carton ready for Mailing.
Price Per doz. **$48.00**

No. 3329X 3-Piece Console Sets
Each Set consists of one "Jug-Time" Clock and 2 Candlesticks
Price-Packed 1 set in mailable carton-Per Doz. Sets **$48.00**

No. 3336X Mantel or Bureau Set
Each Set consists of "Flapper Clock" and 2 Candlesticks
Price-Packed 1 set in mailable carton Per Doz. Sets **$39.00**

NOVELTY "WISE OWL" CLOCK
No. 337L—High Gloss Glazed Majolica Color as above
No. 337P—Soft Pastel semi-gloss Glaze, see set as below
No. 337 is 7¼ in. high and 6½ in. wide. Per Doz.
Weight 5 lbs.
Packed 1 in Carton **Clock Only $48.00**

No. 3325P - BOUDOIR CLOCK SET
Each Set consists of Clock and 2 Candle Holders
Packed one set in carton-made in two finishes:
Weight 6 Pounds Per Doz. Sets
No. 3325L—High Gloss Majolica Ware
No. 3325P Pastel Finish as illustrated **$60.00**

1929 LIST PRICES

61

PORCH AND GARDEN POTTERY

A new line of merit Beautifully modeled and artistically finished. Price is exceptionally low considering value.

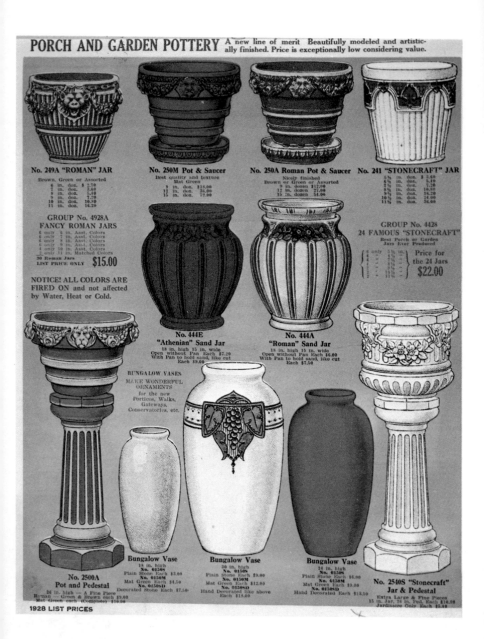

No. 249A "ROMAN" JAR

Brown, Green or Assorted

6 in. doz.	$	2.70
7 in. doz.		3.60
8 in. doz.		5.40
9 in. doz.		7.20
10 in. doz.		10.80
11 in. doz.		16.20

GROUP No. 4928A
FANCY ROMAN JARS

6 only 6 in. Asst. Colors
6 only 7 in. Asst. Colors
6 only 8 in. Asst. Colors
6 only 9 in. Asst. Colors
4 only 10 in. Asst. Colors
2 only 11 in. Matched Colors

30 Roman Jars
LIST PRICE ONLY **$15.00**

**NOTICE! ALL COLORS ARE
FIRED ON** and not affected
by Water, Heat or Cold.

No. 250M Pot & Saucer
Best quality and texture
Mat Green

9 in. doz.	$18.00
12 in. doz.	36.00
15 in. doz.	72.00

**No. 444E
"Athenian" Sand Jar**
18 in. high 15 in. wide
Open without Pan Each $7.20
With Pan to hold sand, like cut
Each $9.60

BUNGALOW VASES
MAKE WONDERFUL
ORNAMENTS
for the new
Porticos, Walks,
Gateways,
Conservatories, etc.

No. 250A Roman Pot & Saucer
Nicely finished
Brown or Green or Assorted

9 in. dozen	$12.00
12 in. dozen	27.00
15 in. dozen	54.00

**No. 444A
"Roman" Sand Jar**
18 in. high 15 in. wide
Open without Pan Each $6.00
With Pan to hold sand, like cut
Each $7.50

No. 241 "STONECRAFT" JAR

5½ in. doz.	$	3.60
6½ in. doz.		7.20
7½ in. doz.		7.20
8½ in. doz.		10.80
9½ in. doz.		18.20
10½ in. doz.		24.00
11½ in. doz.		36.00

GROUP No. 4428
24 FAMOUS "STONECRAFT"
Best Porch or Garden
Jars Ever Produced

6 only 5½ in.
6 only 6½ in.
4 only 7½ in.
4 only 8½ in.
2 only 9½ in.
1 only 10½ in.
1 only 11½ in.

Price for
the 24 Jars
$22.00

**No. 2500A
Pot and Pedestal**
26 in. high — A Fine Piece
Roman — Green & Brown each $9.00
Mat Green each (Complete) $10.50

Bungalow Vase
18 in. high
No. 0150S
Plain Stone Each $3.00
No. 0150M
Mat Green Each $4.50
No. 0150SD
Decorated Stone Each $7.50

Bungalow Vase
20 in. high
No. 0150S
Plain Stone Each $9.00
No. 0150M
Mat Green Each $12.00
No. 0150SD
Hand Decorated like above
Each $18.00

Bungalow Vase
24 in. high
No. 0150M
Plain Stone Each $6.00
No. 0150M
Mat Green Each $9.00
No. 0150SD
Hand Decorated Each $13.50

**No. 2540S "Stonecraft"
Jar & Pedestal**
Extra Large & Fine Pieces
15 in. Jar, 24 in. Ped. Each $16.00
Jardinere Only Each $5.40

1928 LIST PRICES

"MODERNE" "KOLORKRAFT" VASES

No. 0153KX
3 in. Vase doz. $2.60

No. 0154KX
4 in. Vase doz. $5.00

No. 0159KX
9 in. Vase doz. $18.00

No. 0160KX
10 in. Vase doz. $23.50

No. 0155KX
5 in. Vase doz. $7.20

No. 0156KX
6 in. Vase doz. $10.50

No. 0161KX
11 in. Vase doz. $24.00

No. 0162KX
12 in. Vase doz. $27.00

No. 0158KX
6 in. Vase doz. $15.00

No. 0157KX
7 in. Vase doz. $12.00

COLORS — The above line of "Moderne" Kolorkraft Vases may be had in Rose, Blue, Green or Orchid — We advise ordering Assorted and we send Colors Selling Best at time order is received.

"Moderne" Lamp Vase
No. 0105K
6 in. doz. $6.00

"Globe" Lamp Vase
No. 0102K
5½ in. doz. $10.00

"Pyramid" Dec. Vase
No. 0104K
9 in. doz. $18.00

"Pyramid" Lamp Vase
No. 0103K
9 in. doz. $12.00

LAMP VASES- Colors: Rose, Blue, Orchid, Green or Ivory. Any lamp fitted up ready for shade $1.50 each.

"AMARYLLIS" "KOLORKRAFT" VASES
UNIQUE SHAPES — WONDERFUL COLORS

No. 0185KA
3 in. Vase doz. $2.00

No. 0181KA
4½ in. Bowl doz. $2.00

No. 0182KA
2½ in. Vase doz. $2.50

No. 0186KA
4½ in. Bowl doz. $6.00

No. 0189KA
6 in. Vase doz. $5.40

No. 0190KA
6 in. Vase doz. $7.20

No. 0187KA
6 in. Vase doz. $5.40

No. 0191KA
6½ in. Vase doz. $9.60

No. 0192KA
7½ in. Vase doz. $14.40

No. 0193KA
9½ in. Vase doz. $18.20

COLORS: Rose, Green, Orchid, High Gloss Glaze.

"KOLORKRAFT" NOVELTIES

No. 025K
Candlestick
3 in. doz. $1.00

No. 611KA Flower Bowl
Green, Orchid or Rose

4½ in. Any Color doz.	$3.40
5½ in. Any Color doz.	4.50
6½ in. Any Color doz.	7.20
7½ in. Any Color doz.	10.40
8½ in. Any Color doz.	15.00

No. 460K
Wall Vase
7 in. doz. $5.40

No. 026KA
Candlestick
9 in. doz. $5.40

No. 03DK Frog*
Decorated doz. $7.20

Blocks to Match
No. 01K 2 in. doz. $1.80
No. 02K 2½ in. doz. $2.40

"MODERNE" "KOLORKRAFT" JARS
No. 260K

COLORS					EITHER COLOR OR ASSTD.
ROSE	No. 260K	6 in. Jardiniere doz.	$3.40		
ORCHID	No. 260K	7 in. Jardiniere doz.	5.50		
GREEN	No. 260K	8 in. Jardiniere doz.	7.20		
	No. 260K	9 in. Jardiniere doz.	10.50		
	No. 260K	10 in. Jardiniere doz.	15.00		

"AMARYLLIS" "KOLORKRAFT" JARS
No. 252KA

COLORS					EITHER COLOR OR ASSTD.
ROSE	No. 252KA	6½ in. Jardiniere doz.	$3.60		
ORCHID	No. 252KA	7½ in. Jardiniere doz.	4.40		
GREEN	No. 252KA	8½ in. Jardiniere doz.	7.20		
	No. 252KA	9½ in. Jardiniere doz.	10.80		
	No. 252KA	11½ in. Jardiniere doz.	21.00		

PASTEL is produced for the lover of the Beautiful as well as Useful, will match the soft shades of modern kitchens— Many pieces decorated with Tulips in Harmonious Colors.

The
Brush
Pottery
Co.,
Zanesville,
Ohio
U. S. A.

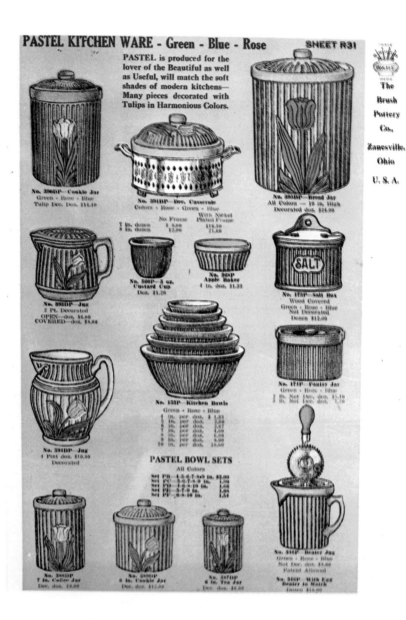

No. 390DP—Cookie Jar
Green - Rose - Blue
Tulip Dec. Doz. $14.40

No. 391DP—Dec. Casserole
Colors - Rose - Green - Blue

	No Frame	With Nickel Plated Frame
7 lb. dozen	$ 8.00	$16.50
8 lb. dozen	12.00	21.60

No. 393DP—Bread Jar
All Colors - 10 in. High
Decorated doz. $24.00

No. 392DP—Jug
2 Pt. Decorated
OPEN—doz. $6.00
COVERED—doz. $8.00

No. 366P—5 oz.
Custard Cup
Doz. $1.20

No. 368P
Apple Baker
4 in. doz. $1.33

No. 173P—Salt Box
Wood Covered
Green - Rose - Blue
Not Decorated
Dozen $12.00

No. 394DP—Jug
4 Pint doz. $10.50
Decorated

No. 133P—Kitchen Bowls
Green - Rose - Blue

4 in. per doz.	$ 1.33
5 in. per doz.	2.00
6 in. per doz.	2.67
7 in. per doz.	4.00
8 in. per doz.	6.00
9 in. per doz.	8.00
10 in. per doz.	10.00

No. 174P—Pantry Jar
Green - Rose - Blue
2 lb. Not Dec. doz. $5.10
3 lb. Not Dec. doz. 7.50

PASTEL BOWL SETS
All Colors

Set PB—4-5-6-7-8-9 in.	$2.00
Set PC—5-6-7-8-9 in.	1.50
Set PD—4-5-6-7-8 in.	1.66
Set PE—5-6-7-8 in.	1.25
Set PF—5-6-7-8-9 in.	1.51

No. 385IP—7 in. Coffee Jar
Dec. doz. $9.00

No. 385IP—6 in. Cookie Jar
Dec. doz. $15.00

No. 385IP—6 in. Tea Jar
Dec. doz. $5.00

No. 346P—Beater Jug
Green - Rose - Blue
Not Dec. doz. $6.00
Patent Allowed

No. 346P—With Egg Beater to Match
Dozen $16.00

The Brush Pottery Co.,
Zanesville,
Ohio
U. S. A.

OUR COMBINATION
FOUNTAINS and BATHS

are artistically modeled — finely finished — hard burned and· will add beauty to any Garden. They are also appreciated by our feathered friends. All are pottery — Not cement. All colors fired — No cold paint used.

TRADE **WARE** MARK

The Brush Pottery Co., Zanesville, Ohio U. S. A.

No. 0251 Ornament only
Frogs & Toad Stool

As shown below—No fittings
Decorated - Green each $10.80
Plain Stone each 9.60
(Above are Patented)

No. 02622 Combination Fountain & Bird Bath

Bath 20 in. Height over all 49 in.
Dec. ROMAN
Green & Tan Finish ea. $30.00
Plain Stone ea. $27.00

No. 200 ORNAMENT

Seal and Ball as illustrated above.
(ornament only)
17 in. high with fittings.
Dec. as shown ea. $12.00
Plain Stone each 10.80

No. 025108—Combination (Patented)
FOUNTAIN, BIRD BATH AND FEEDER
Bath 20 in. Height over all 37 in.
Dec. "Roman" Finish. Green & Tan $24.00
Plain "Stonecraft" Finish, complete 21.60

No. 02625 Combination Fountain & Bird Bath

Bath 20 in. Height over all 47 in.
Dec. ROMAN Green ea. $30.00
Plain Stone ea. 27.00

No. 215 ORNAMENT

Mermaid as illustrated above.
15 in. High
No fittings.
Decorated ea. $10.00
Plain Stone ea. 9.00
Above price is for "Mermaid" only.
Can be used in other Baths- Rock Garden. etc.

"NYMPH" Handled Vases - Artistically Modeled
Beautifully Colored - Art Mat Glazes

"Nymph" Line finished in
Maple-Rose-Green-Blue

The
Brush
Pottery
Co.,
Zanesville,
Ohio
U. S. A.

No. 018-6 in.
Doz. $3.00

No. 721-6 in.
Doz. $4.80

No. 722-7 in.
Doz. $6.00

No. 723-8 in.
Doz. $9.00

No. 724-9 in.
Doz. 9.60

No. 830-10 in.
Doz. $18.00

"FAWN" VASES-Each piece a distinctive creation
"Fawn" Vases finished in Art Vellum
Blue-Green-Maple-Maroon

No. 716 Vase
5 in. high, 6 in. wide
Doz. $6.00

No. 717 Vase
6½ in. high, 6 in. wide
Doz. $9.00

No. 718 Vase
7½ in. high, 8 in. wide
Doz. $21.60

No. 719 Vase
8 in. high, 8 in. wide
Doz. $24.00

EMPRESS LINES - Footed Vases
Artistically Modeled - Beautifully Finished - High Gloss Glazes

No. 703 Vase
5¼ in. high
Dozen $3.60

No. 704 Vase
6 in. high
Dozen $4.50

No. 705 Vase
6 in. high
Dozen $4.50

No. 706 Vase
6 in. high
Dozen $4.50

No. 707 Vase
7 in. high
Dozen $6.00

No. 708 Vase
7 in. high
Dozen $7.20

No. 714 Vase
12 in. high
Dozen $18.00

No. 713 Vase
10¼ in. high
Dozen $14.40

No. 712 Vase
9¼ in. high
Dozen $12.00

No. 711 Vase
9 in. high
Dozen $12.00

No. 710 Vase
8 in. high
Dozen $10.80

No. 709 Vase
8 in. high
Dozen $9.00

NEW "VESTAL" DUO-TONE VASES

**Artistically Modeled - finished in two subdued tones —
soft mat colors: Green - Tan - Old Rose**
furnished as
requested.

No. 725V Vase	No. 726V Vase	No. 727V Vase	No. 728V Vase	No. 729V Vase
4½ in. wide	6 in. wide	7¾ in. wide	7¾ in. wide	5½ in. wide
6 in. high	8 in. high	8½ in. high	9 in. high	10¼ in. high
Either Color	Either Color	Either Color	Either Color	Either Color
Doz. $5.00	Doz. $10.00	Doz. $16.00	Doz. $16.00	Doz. $18.00

GENUINE "ONYX" ART VASES
SPECIAL VALUE

Don't Miss These

No. 050X Vase	No. 060X Vase	No. 062X Vase	No. 063X Vase
Full 6 in. High	Full 8 in. High	Full 10 in. High	Full 12½ in. High
Dozen $4.00	Dozen $7.20	Dozen $13.20	Dozen $18.00

SPECIAL ONYX VASES—High Grade Blue - Green - Brown Onyx Finish!   BIG VALUE!

"ROCKRAFT"

is offered critical purchasers and especially those interested in the distinctive and unusual in pottery creations. It is actually modeled from the rocks themselves, and carries all the veins, corners and irregularities. Our Craftsmen have endeavored to clothe it with two most pleasing finishes. All pieces are made in both Stone and Moss Finish. State "S" for Stone, "M" for Moss.   Price the same.

No. 882S—Bulb Pan
6 in. x 3 in. high
Doz. $15.00

No. 881CM—Pot
4½ x 4½ inch
Doz. $10.80

No. 8812S—Vase
6 inch doz. $18.00

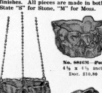

No. 8862M—7 in. Hanging Basket	No. 8862M—Pot	No. 8865M	No. 8810S—Pot	No. 8880S Jardiniere
Doz. $15.00	4 x 4 inch Doz. $6.00	7 in. high doz. $24.00 8 in. high doz. $30.00	4½ x 4½ inch Doz. $10.80	7 inch doz. $24.00 8 inch doz. $30.00

"ROCKRAFT" SPECIAL - Any of the above pieces furnished in Plain
Art Mat Green - LIST PRICE ONE-HALF ABOVE.

"CAMEO" Jars and Jars and Pedestal

No. 273D JARDINIERE
"Duotone" Mat-Green or Tan

7 in. doz. $ 7.20		10 in. doz. $24.00
8 in. doz. 10.80		11 in. doz. 36.00
9 in. doz. 16.20		

No. 273X JARDINIERE
Green - Chocolate - Canary Onyx

7 in. doz. $ 5.00		10 in. doz. $14.40
8 in. doz. 7.20		11 in. doz. 21.60
9 in. doz. 10.80		

No. 2730D POT & PEDESTAL
"Duotone" Mat-Green or Tan
11 in. Jar - 18 in. Ped. - 28 in. High
Either Color - Each $9.00

No. 2730X POT & PEDESTAL
Green - Chocolate - Canary Onyx
11 in. Jar - 18 in. Ped. - 28 in. High
Either Color - Each $7.20

"EMPRESS" Footed Line

No. 698X FOOTED BOWL
Green-Brown-Blue Onyx

4 ½ in. wide, 2 ½ in. opening - doz. $ 3.33
6 in. wide, 4 ½ in. opening - doz. 6.00
7 ½ in. wide, 5 in. opening - doz. 9.60
8 ½ in. wide, 6 in. opening - doz. 14.40

No. 699G URN
Art Mat Glazes - Green-Tan

5 ½ in. wide, 4 in. opening dz. $ 6.00
7 in. wide, 5 ½ in. opening dz. 12.00
9 in. wide, 6 ½ in. opening dz. 21.60
11 ½ in. wide, 8 ½ in. opening dz. 48.00
15 in. wide, 11 in. opening dz. 96.00

No. 699X URN - Green or Brown Onyx

5 ½ in. wide, 4 in. opening dz. $ 6.00
7 in. wide, 5 ½ in. opening dz. 12.00
9 in. wide, 6 ½ in. opening dz. 21.60
11 ½ in. wide, 8 ½ in. opening dz. 48.00
15 in. wide, 11 in. opening dz. 96.00

No. 269KX BALL JAR-Footed
7 in. high, 8 in. wide
Beautiful Kolorkraft Glazes
Per dozen $15.00

No. 6990 URN & PEDESTAL
27 in. high. Urn 15 inches wide
Onyx-Green or Brown - Each $16.00

"JETWOOD"

"JETWOOD" A mirror-like Jet Black decoration on beautifully shaded background representing twilight in the woodland. Hand decorated each piece different and each a distinct work of art. Very hard burned.

No. 050W Vase 6 in. high doz. $30.00   No. 049W Vase 8 in. high doz. $45.00   No. 047W Bud Vase 10 in. high doz. $45.00   No. 044W Vase 10 in. high doz. $50.00   No. 045W Vase 11 in. high doz. $60.00   No. 046W Vase 12 in. high doz. $72.00

LAMP BASES—Any Vase on this page fitted with hole for lamp base at $6.00 per dozen additional

"JETWOOD" Gift Group No. 3323W
1 each of the eleven "Jetwood" Vases and 1 No. 055W Fern and liner. **$41.67**
12 Hand Decorated "Jetwood" Pieces

No. 055W Fern 5 in. with liner doz. $27.00   No. 052W Vase 4 in. high $18.00   No. 041W Vase 6 in. doz. $21.60   No. 041W Vase 8 in. doz. $30.00   No. 041W Vase 10 in. doz. $45.00   No. 041W Vase 12 in. doz. $60.00

No. 01W Bowl 4 in. doz. $12.00   No. 01W Bowl 5 in. doz. $18.00   No. 01W Bowl 6 in. doz. $24.00   No. 01W Bowl 7 in. doz. $36.00   No. 01W Bowl 8 in. doz. $54.00

Hand Dec. Group No. 3423W
2 only No. 01W 4 in. Bowl, 5 in., 6 in., 7 in., 8 in.   2 No. 030W Candlestick, 2 No. 032W   2 only No. 02W Block, 2 only No. 05W, 1 only No. 01W Lily Leaf, 1 only No. 03W Frog
18 Pieces Hand Decorated "Jetwood" $30.00

No. 03W Frog Dozen $15.00   No. 01W Lily Leaf Dozen $12.60   Jetwood Block No. 02W 2 in. doz. $6.00 No. 05W 3½ in. doz. $9.00

No. 032W Candlestick 10 in. doz. $45.00   No. 030W Candlestick 7 in. doz. $24.00

No. 240W Jardiniere 7½ in. Jetwood doz. $30.00   No. 240W Jardiniere 8½ in. Jetwood $45.00   No. 240W Jardiniere 9½ in. Jetwood doz. $60.00   No. 240W Jardiniere 10½ in. Jetwood doz. $80.00

1923 LIST PRICES

70

An innovation in Art Pottery—Body finished in rich Color Glazes—Decorations in harmonious colors—Extremely hard burned— Each Piece a work of Art—Hand Decorated

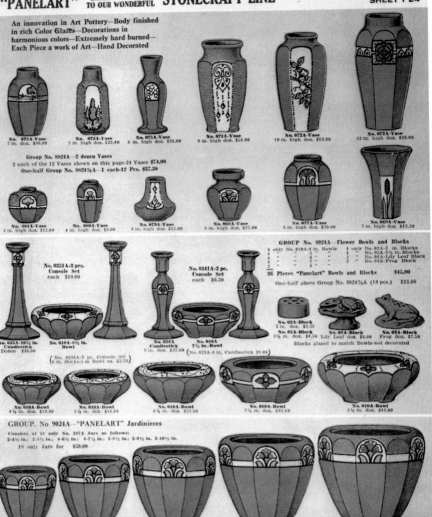

No. 078A-Vase
7 in. doz. $26.00

No. 076A-Vase
7 in. high doz. $32.40

No. 075A-Vase
8 in. high doz. $36.00

No. 071A-Vase
9 in. high doz. $54.00

No. 072A-Vase
10 in. high doz. $63.00

No. 073A-Vase
12 in. high doz. $90.00

Group No. 8824A—2 dozen Vases
2 each of the 12 Vases shown on this page-24 Vases $74.00
One-half Group No. 8824½A—1 each-12 Pcs. $37.50

No. 081A-Vase
3 in. high doz. $12.00

No. 080A-Vase
4 in. high doz. $9.00

No. 079A-Vase
4 in. high doz. $15.00

No. 068A-Vase
5 in. high doz. $27.00

No. 077A-Vase
6 in. high doz. $36.00

No. 069A-Vase
7 in. high doz. $43.20

No. 0251A-3 pcs.
Console Set
each $10.00

No. 0341A-3 pc.
Console Set
each $6.30

GROUP No. 8924A—Flower Bowls and Blocks

6 only No. 010A-4 in. Bowls	4 only No. 02A-3 in. Blocks
6 " " 5 " "	4 " No. 05A-3½ in. Blocks
6 " " 6 " "	2 " No. 04A-Lily Leaf Block
2 " " 7 " "	2 " No. 03A-Frog Block

36 Pieces "Panelart" Bowls and Blocks $45.00

One-half above Group No. 8924½A (18 pcs.) $23.00

No. 02A-Block
2 in. doz. $2.25

No. 05A-Block
3½ in. doz. $4.50

No. 04A-Block
Lily Leaf doz. $6.00

No. 03A-Block
Frog doz. $7.50

Blocks glazed to match Bowls-not decorated

No. 033A-10½ in.
Candlestick
Dozen $36.00

No. 010A-8½ in.
Bowl

(No. 0291A-3 pc. Console Set
6 in. Sticks-5 in. Bowl ea. $2.76)

No. 034A
Candlestick
9 in. doz. $27.00

No. 010A
7½ in-Bowl

(No. 029A-6 in. Candlestick $9.00)

No. 010A-Bowl
4½ in. doz. $10.80

No. 010A-Bowl
5½ in. doz. $14.40

No. 010A-Bowl
6½ in. doz. $21.60

No. 010A-Bowl
7½ in. doz. $32.40

No. 010A-Bowl
8½ in. doz. $45.00

GROUP. No 9024A—"PANELART" Jardinieres

Consists of 18 only No. 247A Jars as follows:
2-4½ in.; 2-5½ in.; 4-6½ in.; 4-7½ in.; 2-8½ in.; 2-9½ in. 2-10½ in.
18 only Jars for $59.00

No. 247A-Jardiniere
4½ in. doz. $12.50
          27.00

No. 247A-Jardiniere
5½ in. doz. $18.00
7½ in. doz. $36.00

No. 247A-Jardiniere
8½ in. doz. $45.00

No. 247A-Jardiniere
9½ in. doz. $63.00

No. 247A-Jardiniere
10½ in. doz. $90.00

24 LIST PRICES

SHEET M 25

"COLONIAL MAT"

A New Finish of Rare Beauty-Hard Burned Body-Rich Colored Glazes-Green, Fawn and Blue-Soft Velvet texture-An artistic ware at an exceedingly low price. All pieces furnished in either color except umbrella stand.

1925 LIST PRICES — COLONIAL MAT

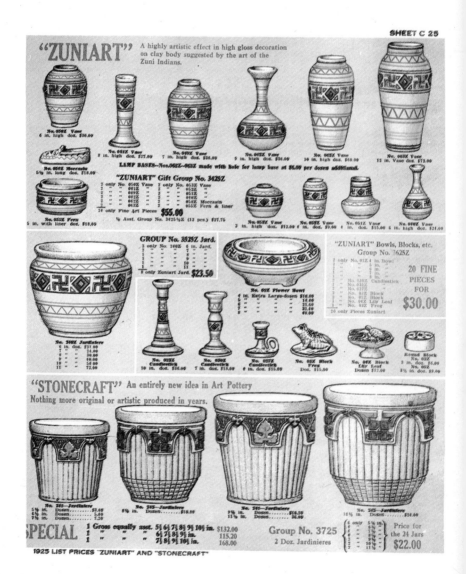

"ZUNIART"

A highly artistic effect in high gloss decoration on clay body suggested by the art of the Zuni Indians.

No. 050Z Vase
6 in. high doz. $30.00

No. 054Z Moccasin
5½ in. long doz. $18.00

No. 048Z Vase
5 in. high doz. $27.00

No. 049Z Vase
7 in. high doz. $36.00

No. 047Z Vase
9 in. high doz. $36.00

No. 055Z Vase
10 in. high doz. $60.00

No. 053Z Vase
12 in. Vase doz. $72.00

LAMP BASES—Nos.062Z–065Z made with hole for lamp base at $6.00 per dozen additional.

"ZUNIART" Gift Group No. 3425Z

No. 055Z Fern
5 in. with liner doz. $18.00

3 only No. 050Z Vase
3 " " 061Z "
3 " " 049Z "
3 " " 042Z "
3 " " 067Z "
3 " " 063Z "

3 only No. 053Z Vase
3 " " 062Z "
3 " " 061Z "
3 " " 040Z "
3 " " 054Z Moccasin
3 " " 055Z Fern & liner

24 only Fine Art Pieces **$55.00**

½ Asst. Group No. 3425½Z (12 pcs.) $27.75

No. 056Z Vase
3 in. high doz. $12.00

No. 059Z Vase
4 in. high doz. $9.00

No. 051Z Vase
6 in. high doz. $15.00

No. 040Z Vase
6 in. high doz. $24.00

GROUP No. 3535Z Jard.

3 only No. 240Z 6 in. Jard.
1 " " 7 " "
1 " " 8 " "
1 " " 9 " "
1 " " 10 " "
1 " " 11 " "

8 only Zuniart Jard. **$23.50**

No. 240Z Jardiniere
6 in. doz. $21.00
7 " " 24.00
8 " " 30.00
9 " " 48.00
10 " " 54.00
11 " " 72.00

No. 01Z Flower Bowl
6 in. Extra Large–dozen $10.00
7 " " " 14.00
8 " " " 21.00
9 " " " 32.00
10 " " " 48.00

No. 03Z Candlestick
10 in. doz. $36.00

No. 05Z Candlestick
7 in. doz. $18.00

No. 027Z Candlestick
6 in. doz. $15.00

No. 03Z Block Frog
Doz. $15.00

"ZUNIART" Bowls, Blocks, etc.

Group No. 3625Z

2 only No. 01Z 4 in. Bowl
1 " " 6 in. "
1 " " 8 in. "
1 " " No. 030Z Candlestick
1 " " No. 03Z Z
1 " " No. 027Z
1 " " No. 3Z Block
1 " " No. 05Z Block
1 " " No. 04Z Lily Leaf
1 " " No. 03Z Frog

16 only Pieces Zuniart

20 FINE PIECES FOR $30.00

No. 04Z Block Lily Leaf
Dozen $12.00

Round Block
No. 02Z
3 in. doz. $6.00
No. 05Z
3½ in. doz. $9.00

"STONECRAFT"

An entirely new idea in Art Pottery

Nothing more original or artistic produced in years.

No. 241—Jardiniere
5½ in. Dozen......$9.60
6½ " Dozen...... 5.40
7½ " Dozen...... 7.20

No. 242—Jardiniere
8½ in. Dozen......$10.80

No. 240—Jardiniere
9½ in. Dozen......$16.20
11½ " Dozen...... 26.00

No. 242—Jardiniere
10½ in. Dozen......$24.00

SPECIAL

1 Gross equally asst. 5½ 6½ 7½ 8½ 9½ 10½ in. $132.00
1 " " " 6½ 7½ 8½ 9½ in. 115.20
1 " " " 7½ 8½ 9½ 10½ in. 168.00

Group No. 3725
2 Doz. Jardinieres

6 only 5½ in.
4 " 6½ "
4 " 7½ "
4 " 8½ "
2 " 9½ "
2 " 10 "
2 " 11 "

Price for the 24 Jars **$22.00**

1925 LIST PRICES "ZUNIART" AND "STONECRAFT"

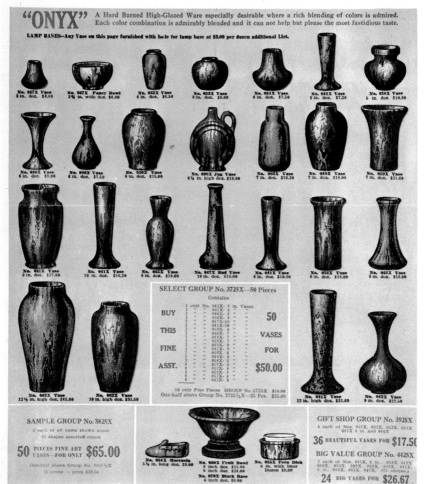

"ONYX" A Hard Burned High-Glazed Ware especially desirable where a rich blending of colors is admired. Each color combination is admirably blended and it can not help but please the most fastidious taste.

LAMP BASES--Any Vase on this page furnished with hole for lamp base at $3.00 per dozen additional List.

"ONYX" Novelties, Console Sets, Flower Bowls Candlesticks and Jardinieres.

SHEET P 25

"JUG-TIME" NOVELTY ART CLOCK AND CONSOLE SET

NEW UMBRELLA STAND

BEAUTIFUL
UNIQUE
USEFUL

No. 333X "JUG-TIME" Clock

Great for Regular Sale, Gifts Presents, Premiums, Carnivals etc.

DESCRIPTION— Shape like a Handled Flat Grecian Jug, 6¾ inches high, 5¾ inches wide, 2¼ inches thick. Made of Fancy Onyx Pottery, Burned hard, in assorted or choice of three colors — Red Onyx, Blue Onyx, Green Onyx. Clock is 2½ inches set in the middle of the Jug—White Dial—Nickel trimmings. Works enclosed in dust-proof Cap. Stem Wind. Stem set, and regulated from the back.

PACKING— Each Clock packed in individual mailing carton, six cartons in shipping carton. Weight individually 2 pounds 6 in carton 18 pounds. Size of individual carton 2½x3½x9¾, shipping carton 10x13x15 inches.

Patented Oct. 21, 1924
No. 333X "JUG-TIME" Clock
As decribed above packed 1 in carton
Blue, Green or Red Onyx
per doz. **$36.00**
Cartons are mailable.

No. 3329X 3-Piece Console Set

No. 3329X 3-Piece Console Sets
Consist of one Jug-Time Clock and 2 No. 029X 6 in. Colonial Candlestick to match in style and color.

No. 3329X 3-Piece Console Set

Unique, Beautiful and attractive to every class of people-sells on sight-made in three colors, Red Blue and Green Onyx Ware.

PACKING— Each set packed in individual carton mailable at 5 pounds. Excellent for premiums and regular sale.

No. 3329X 3-Piece Console Sets
Packed 1 set in Carton doz. **$48.00**
Furnished in Red, Blue or Green onyx or assorted as desired.

No. 71X Umbrella Stand
20¼ in. high-9½ in. Wide
Furnished in Red, Blue, or Green Onyx
Doz. either color **$72.00**

No. 01X Bowl
4 in. doz. $3.00

No. 01X Bowl
5 in. doz. $6.00

No. 01X Bowl
6 in. doz. $10.80

No. 01X Bowl
7 in. doz. $15.00

No. 01X Bowl
8 in. doz. $22.50

GROUP NO. 4025X—FLOWER BOWLS AND BLOCKS

12 Only No. 01X 4 in. Bowls
8 " " 5 "
6 " " 6 "
4 " " 7 "
4 " " 8 "

8 Only No. 02X Block to fit 1 in Bowls
8 " 05X " 6 "
4 " 04X " 7 "
4 " 01X " 8 "

60 Pieces ONYX Bowls and Blocks **$35.00**
One-half above Group No. 4025½X-30 Pcs. **$17.50**

No. 03X Frog
Dozen $7.50

No. 04X Lily Leaf
Dozen $6.60

No. 02X Disk Flower Block
3 in. doz. $2.25

No. 05X Disk Flower Block
3½ in. doz. $4.50

No. 032X Candlestick
10½ in. doz. $18.00

No. 033X Candlestick
9 in. doz. $13.50

No. 030X Candlestick
7 in. doz. $9.00

No. 029X Candlestick
6 in. doz. $5.40

No. 028X Candlestick
4 in. doz. $3.00

No. 027X Candlestick
4 in. doz. $3.60

GROUP NO. 4125X—"ONYX" Candlesticks

12 only No. 032X- 4 inch
12 " " 027X- 4 "
12 " " 030X- 7 "
12 " " 033X- 9 "
12 " " 032X-10½ "
60

60 Fine Pieces $36.00

One-half above Group No. 4125½X -30 Pcs. $18.00

"ONYX" Jardinieres

GROUP No. 4225X—3 doz.
6 each No. 240X-6¼ and 7¼ in.
4 " " " 8¼, 9¼, 10¼ in.
24 assorted colors **$35.00**
½ above Group No. 4225½X $17.75

GROUP No. 4325X—30 Jars
10 only 6¼ in. No. 240X
8 " " 7¼ "
4 " " 8¼ "
4 " " 9¼ "
4 " " 10¼ "
30 only asst. colors **$33.33**
½ above Group No. 4325½X $16.67

No. 240X Jardiniere
6 in. either color doz. $7.20
7 in. either color doz. 9.00

No. 240X Jardiniere
8 in. either color doz. $10.80
9 in. either color doz. 16.20

No. 240X Jardiniere
10 in. either color doz. $25.20
11 in. either color doz. 36.00

1925 LIST PRICES

"ART VELLUM" Texture of ancient-parchment—rich harmonizing colors in soft pleasing effects.

VASES for every Purse and Purpose

No. 041V—6-in. Vase
Dozen $7.20

No. 041V—8-in. Vase
Dozen $10.80

No. 041V—10-inch
Dozen $16.20

No. 041V—12-inch
Dozen $21.60

No. 047V—9 in. Vase
Dozen $22.50

No 053V—10-in. Vase
Dozen $31.50

No. 053V—12-in. Vase
Dozen $45.00

GIFT SHOP GROUP NO. 4525V
2 each of the 15 vases shown on this sheet
2½ Doz. Art Vellum Vases

$40.00

One-half above No. 4525½V—15 pcs. $20.00

FOR LAMP BASES
Any Vase on this page furnished with hole in bottom
for lamp base-add $3.00 per dos. List

No. 052V
4 inch
Doz. $4.50

No. 055V
3 inch
Doz. $6.00

No. 051V
4 inch
Doz. $7.50

No. 010V—6-in. Vase
Dozen $7.50

No. 048V—6-in. Vase
Dozen $9.00

No. 050V—6-inch
Dozen....$15.00

No. 049V—7-inch
Dozen....$18.00

No. 037V—10-in Bud Vase
Dozen $18.00

A FINE LINE OF POPULAR CANDLESTICKS

No. 032V
Candlestick 10-in.
Dozen $18.00

No. 033V
Candlestick 8½-in.
Dozen $13.50

No. 030V
Candlestick 7-in.
Dozen $9.00

No. 029V
Candlestick, 6-in.
Dozen $5.40

No. 027V
Candlestick 4-in.
Dozen $3.60

No. 028V
Candlestick 4-in.
Dozen $3.00

No. 02V
3 in. Block
Doz. $2.25

No. 05V
3½ in. Block
Doz. $4.50

No. 04V
Lily Leaf
Doz. $6.00

No. 01V—Flower Bowl
4½ in. Either color Doz. $ 5.00
5½ " " " 6.00
6½ " " " 10.50
7½ " " " 15.00
8½ " " " 22.50

No. 03V
Frog
Doz. $7.50

Group No. 4625V 3 Doz. Candlesticks

8 only No. 028V—4 in.	6 only No. 030V— 7 in.
8 " " 027V—4 in.	4 " " 032V—8½ in.
6 " " 029V—6 in.	4 " " 033V—10½ "

36 ONLY GROUP No. 4625V   **$22.00**

Group No. 4725V 3 Doz. Bowls & Blocks

6 only No. 01V—4½ in. Bowls	4 only No. 02V—3 in. Blocks
6 " " 01V—5½ "	4 " " 05V—3½ in.
4 " " 01V—6½ "	4 " " 04V—Lily
4 " " 01V—7½ "	2 " " 03V—Frog
2 " " 01V—8½ "	

26 PIECE FANCY BOWLS & BLOCKS   **$23.00**

Group No. 4825V   JARDINIERES

| 4 only No. 210V— 6 in. Jardinieres |
| 4 " " " 7 in. " |
| 4 " " " 8 in. " |
| 4 " " " 9 in. " |
| 2 " " " 10 in. " |
| 2 " " " 11 in. " |

20 ONLY JARDINIERES   **$24.00**

No. 210V—Jardiniere
6 in. Either Color doz. $ 7.20
7 " " " 9.00
8 " " " 10.80
9 " " " 16.20
10 " " " 25.20
11 " " " 36.00

JARDINIERES --

THREE DISTINCT NOVELTIES—ALL HIGH GRADE—MEDIUM PRICED AND SHOULD BE IN EVERY STORE.—ALL COLORS FIRED ON.—EVERY PIECE HIGHLY GLAZED INSIDE AND OUT.—RICH, BEAUTIFUL COLORS.

GROUP No. 125H - 2 dozen   **$15.67** LIST
4 each 6, 7, 8, 9, 10 & 11 inch
2 DOZEN No. 243H JARS

GROUP No. 225H - 3 dozen   **$15.00** LIST
9 each 6, 7, 8 and 9 inch
3 DOZ. No. 243H JARDINIERES

GROUP No. 325H - 2 dozen   **$14.00** LIST
6 each 7, 8, 9 and 10 inch
2 DOZEN No. 243H JARDINIERES

GROUP No. 425H - 2 dozen   **$20.00** LIST
6 each 8, 9, 10 and 11 inch
2 DOZ. No. 243H JARDINIERES

No. 243N "NUGLAZ" JARDINIERES

4½ in. actual measure asst. colors doz. $ 2.40

6	"	"	"	3.00
7	"	"	"	4.00
8	"	"	"	6.00
9	"	"	"	9.00
10	"	"	"	12.00
11	"	"	"	18.00

GROUP No. 525N - 2 dozen   **$16.67** LIST
4 each 6, 7, 8, 9, 10 & 11 inch
2 DOZ. No. 243N JARDINIERES

GROUP No. 625N - 3 dozen   **$16.20** LIST
9 each 6, 7, 8 and 9 inch
3 DOZ. No. 243N JARDINIERES

GROUP No. 725N - 2 dozen   **$15.00** LIST
6 each 7, 8, 9 and 10 inch
2 DOZ. No. 243N JARDINIERES

GROUP No. 825N - 2 dozen   **$22.00** LIST
6 each 8, 9, 10 and 11 inch
2 DOZ. No. 243N JARDINIERES

No. 243H "HIGH-GLOSS Jardinieres

4½ in. actual measure asst. colors doz. $ 2.25

6	"	"	"	2.75
7	"	"	"	3.75
8	"	"	"	5.40
9	"	"	"	8.10
10	"	"	"	10.80
11	"	"	"	16.20

No. 244N "NUGLAZ" JARDINIERES

6 in. actual measure asst. colors doz. $ 3.60

7	"	"	"	4.80
8	"	"	"	7.20
9	"	"	"	10.80
10	"	"	"	15.00
11	"	"	"	21.00

GROUP No. 925N - 2 dozen   **$20.00** LIST
4 each 6, 7, 8, 9, 10 and 11 inch
2 DOZ. No. 244N JARDINIERES

GROUP No. 1025N - 3 dozen   **$19.80** LIST
9 each 6, 7, 8 and 9 inch
3 DOZ. No. 244N JARDINIERES

GROUP No. 1125N - 2 dozen   **$18.90** LIST
6 each 7, 8, 9 and 10 inch
2 DOZ. No. 244N JARDINIERES

GROUP No. 1225N - 2 dozen   **$27.00** LIST
6 each 8, 9, 10 and 11 inch
2 DOZ. No. 244N JARDINIERES

SPECIAL REDUCED PRICE GROUPS FOR THE THRIFTY BUYER

GROUP No. 1325 - 3 dz. Assorted   **$25.00** LIST
2 ea. No. 243N-6, 7, 8, 9, 10 & 11 in.
2 ea. No. 243H-6, 7, 8, 9, 10 & 11 in.
2 ea. No. 244N-6, 7, 8, 9, 10 & 11 in.
3 DOZ. FANCY JARDINIERES

GROUP No. 1425 - 3 dozen assorted   **$17.00** LIST
3 each No. 243H-6, 7, 8, 9 inch
3 each No. 243N-6, 7, 8, 9 inch
3 each No. 244N-6, 7, 8, 9 inch
3 DOZ. FANCY JARDINIERES

GROUP No. 1525 - 3 dozen assorted   **$24.00** LIST
3 each No. 243H 7, 8, 9, 10 inch
3 each No. 243N 7, 8, 9, 10 inch
3 each No. 244N 7, 8, 9, 10 inch
3 DOZ. FANCY JARDINIERES

1925 LIST PRICES - JARDINIERES

"JEWEL" Beautifully colored high gloss jeweled designs hand wrought on new mat body.

SHEET J 25

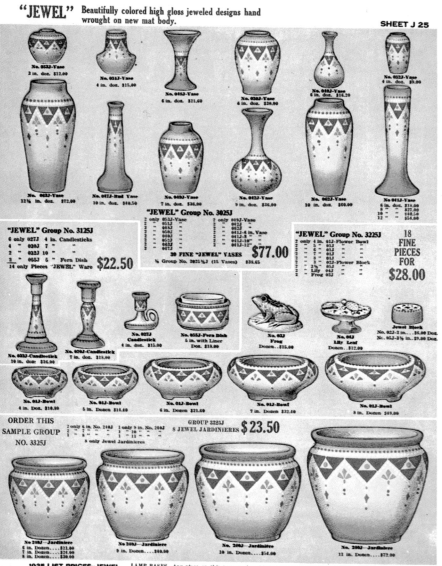

1925 LIST PRICES–JEWEL   LAMP BASES–Any piece on this page made with hole for Lamp Base at $6.00 per Dozen additional List

78

A NEW AND OUTSTANDING EXAMPLE OF THE POTTER'S ART

SHEET K 25

"KRAKLE-KRAFT"

AN ABSOLUTELY UNIQUE ART POTTERY.

Nothing like it made in America. This new ware is produced after several years experimenting with Crackle Bodies and Glazes and is not only Artistic and Interesting from this standpoint but every piece is hard-burned, perfectly glazed and a Beautiful Ornament or Utility Article worth a place in the most elegantly furnished apartment. No collection of Art Pottery is complete without this new ware.

79

INDEX

Aegean Inlaid 41,44
Amaryllis Kolorkraft 63
Arbor 52
Art Vellum 76
Athenian 62
Baby Line 40,41
Basketweave 48
Beautirose 42
Birds, Bees, Butterflies 51,52
Blended Basket 43,44
Blended Glaze 12,17-24, 37,38,54
Blue Birds 41,49
Blue Decorated Bristol 26,28,30,48
Bon-Ton 44,45
Bookends 59
Bruco Toilet Set 52
Bug Door Stop 58
Bungalow Vases 62
Butter Jars 28,31,32,47,48,60
Cacti 59
Card Table Accessories 59
Cameo 69
Candlesticks 41,72,75,76
Cleo 41,44
Clocks 59,61,75
Cobalt Blue 40
Colonial Mat 72
Combinets and Chambers 27,30,40,50
Corn Line 14,16,26,27,34,41
Cuspidors 9,10,13,26,31,40,48,49
Dandy-line 47
Dresden Ware 42
Dutch 57,60
Egyptian 13,55
Empress 67,69
Fawn 67
Fireclay Cooking Ware 28,31,48
Fleur-de-Lis 49
Flora 42
Floradora 59
Florastone 56
Grape Ware 34,49
Grape Jug 60
Green-On-Ivory 27,29,31,40
High-gloss 77
Ivotint 43
Jetwood 70
Jewell 78
KolorKraft 60,63
KolorKraft Kitchenware 60
Krakle-Kraft 79

Lamp Vases 63
Lawn Ornaments 65,66
Liberty Bell 29
Lotus 53
Loy-Nel-Art 5,9,41,44
Majolica 58,59
Marble Ware 25,43,44
Mat Green 11,12,13,41
Moderne KolorKraft 63
Money Banks 27,44
Monochrome 53
Moss Green 44
Mottled Glaze 32,48
Mt. Pelee 4
Mystic Radio Set 61
Navarre Faience 6,39
Novelty Heads 44
Nuglaze 77
Nurock 47
Nymph 67
Oakleaf 43
Old Ivory 14,15
Old Mill 52
Olympia 6
Onyx 17,37,68,74,75
Oriental Ware 36
Our Lucile 50
Pitchers 18,26,31,47,48,49
Panel Art 71
Pastel Kitchenware 64
Patriotic Bee 52
Peacock 47,48
Red Burned Flower Pots 28
Rockcraft 68
Roman 62
Roman Decorated 42
Rosewood 5,6
Salt Box 32,47,48,52,60,64
Silken Mat Green 39
Stone Craft 62,73
Stoneware 32,48
Sylvan 45,54
Uncle Sams Hat 52
Venitian 35,42,59
Vestal 68
Vista 53
Vogue 46,51,53
Willow Ware 48,50
Wise Birds 58,65
Woodland 35,36,41,44
Zuniart 73